Top 25 locator map
(continues on inside
back cover)
◄

CityPack
Lisbon *Top 25*

TIM JEPSON

If you have any comments
or suggestions for this guide
you can contact the editor at
Citypack@theAA.com

AA Publishing
Find out more about AA Publishing and the wide
range of services the AA provides by visiting our
website at *www.theAA.com/bookshop*

About This Book

KEY TO SYMBOLS

ORGANIZATION

This guide is divided into six chapters:
- Planning Ahead, Getting There
- Living Lisbon—Lisbon Now, Lisbon Then, Time to Shop, Out and About, Walks, Lisbon by Night
- Lisbon's Top 25 Sights
- Lisbon's Best—best of the rest
- Where To—detailed listings of restaurants, hotels, shops, and nightlife
- Travel Facts—practical information

In addition, easy-to-read side panels provide extra facts and snippets, highlights of places to visit and invaluable practical advice.

The colours of the tabs on the page corners match the colours of the triangles aligned with the chapter names on the contents page opposite.

MAPS

The fold-out map in the wallet at the back of this book is a comprehensive street plan of Lisbon. The first (or only) grid reference given for each attraction refers to this map. **The Top 25 locator map** found on the inside front and back covers of the book itself is for quick reference. It shows the Top 25 sights, described on pages 26–50, which are clearly plotted by number (**1**–**25**, not page number) across the city. The second map reference given for the Top 25 Sights refers to this map.

Contents

Planning Ahead

WHEN TO GO

Lisbon's hottest and busiest months are July and August; many of the city's inhabitants take their holiday then so some shops and restaurants may be shut. The best months to visit are April, May, June, September and October, when the city is less busy and the weather is bright and mild. Hotels are also quieter in these months.

TIME

Portugal observes the same time as Britain, five hours ahead of New York, 8 hours ahead of Los Angeles.

AVERAGE DAILY MAXIMUM TEMPERATURES

JAN	FEB	MAR	APR	MAY	JUN	JUL	AUG	SEP	OCT	NOV	DEC
57°F	59°F	63°F	67°F	71°F	77°F	81°F	82°F	79°F	72°F	63°F	58°F
14°C	15°C	17°C	20°C	21°C	25°C	27°C	28°C	26°C	22°C	17°C	15°C

Spring (March–May) Often mild and sunny. Rainfall is high in March but decreases quickly in April and May.

Summer (June–September) Hot and dry, but temperatures are tempered by cooling sea breezes. Rain is rare in July and August, but there may be thunderstorms.

Autumn (October–November) Temperatures remain good, with many balmy days, and often clear skies, but rain picks up in October and November.

Winter (December–February) Lisbon bears the brunt of wet, Atlantic depressions and rainfall is highest in December and January, with February a littler drier.

WHAT'S ON

February/March *Carnival celebrations*: Parades, parties and fancy dress.

March/April *Calvary Procession*: Through the Graça district on Good Friday. Easter celebrations throughout the city.

April *Carnation Revolution*: Celebrations to commemorate 25 April 1974.

Bullfighting season: Starts at Campo Pequeno, and continues until October.

May *Annual Book Fair*: Held in the Parque Eduardo VII for three weeks.

Pilgrimage: The first annual pilgrimage to Fátima (13 May).

June *Major feast days*: 13 June (St. Anthony); 24 June (St. John); 29 June (St. Peter). The *Festas dos Santos* (Festivals of the Saints) take place on and around these three days.

Sintra Festival: Classical music in Sintra's churches and palaces (June and July).

Flea Market: At Sintra (29 June).

July *International Summer Jazz Festival*: Organized by the Calouste Gulbenkian Foundation.

Festa de Colete Encarnado: ("Red Waistcoat Fair") in Vila Franca da Xira, 32km (20 miles) from Lisbon, with folk events and a bull-run through the streets. A similar event, the Feira de Outubro, takes place in October.

August *Handicrafts Fair*: Held in Cascais and Estoril.

September *Opera Season*: Starts at the Teatro Nacional de São Carlos and runs to June. Also the start of the football season.

October *Pilgrimage*: The second annual pilgrimage to Fátima (13 October).

Lisbon Online

www.carris.pt
Carries full details of the tram and bus routes run by Carris, the company responsible for the Aerobus airport shuttle and most other public transport within the city. Also has pages devoted to its various city sightseeing tours.

www.metrolisboa.pt
An excellent site (with English section) with all you need to know about routes, tickets and more on the Lisbon metro system.

www.ana-aeroportas.pt
Visit the Lisbon section of Portugal's official airport website for good information on all aspects of the city's Portela airport, plus other useful tourist information.

www.portugalinsite.pt
The official site of the Portuguese trade and tourism organization with tourist information on the country as a whole, including Lisbon.

www.paginasamarelas.pt
The Portuguese version of the Yellow Pages also contains useful listings in English.

www.ccb.pt
The site of the Cultural Centre of Belém provides information on forthcoming concerts, exhibitions and other events, as well as highlighting other aspects of the centre's work.

www.parquedasnacoes.pt
An all-embracing site for the attractions, events and activities at the vast Parque das Nações, the former 1998 Expo site.

www.ipmuseus.pt
An official site that covers most of Portugal's museums, with links to individual galleries.

www.dn.pt
You don't need a good grasp of Portuguese to follow the listings on the website of the *Diario de Notícias*, the Lisbon-based daily newspaper.

GOOD TRAVEL SITES

www.atl-turismolisboa.pt
The official site of the Lisbon tourist office with comprehensive details of hotels, restaurants, transport, museums and other attractions (in English).

www.fodors.com
A travel-planning site. You can research prices and weather; book tickets, cars and rooms and ask fellow travellers questions; links to other sites.

CYBERCAFÉS

Pronto Net
Part of the tourist office. Quick and convenient but more expensive than most of the city's cybercafés.
✚ J8; blV ✉ Lisbon Welcome Centre, Praça do Comércio ☎ 210 312 810 ◷ Daily 9–8 📱 €1.50 for 15 min

Cyberbica
In the Chiado district south of the Teatro Nacional de São Carlos. Inexpensive.
✚ H8; all ✉ Rua dos Duques de Bragança 7 ☎ 213 225 004 ◷ Mon–Sat 11am–midnight 📱 €0.75 for 15 min.

Getting There

INSURANCE

Check your insurance policy and buy any necessary supplements. EU nationals receive free emergency medical treatment with the relevant documentation (form E111 for Britons) but full travel insurance is still advised and is vital for all other travellers.

MONEY

The euro (€) is the official currency of Portugal. Notes in denominations of 5, 10, 20, 50, 100, 200, and 500 euros, and coins in denominations of 1, 2, 5, 10, 20, and 50 cents, and 1 and 2 euros, were introduced in 2002.

€10

€50

€200

€500

ARRIVING

Internal and international flights use Lisbon's Portela Airport 7km (4 miles) north of the city. The Arrivals hall has a tourist information office, car-rental desks and restaurants. Left luggage is available on Level 2 of the P2 car park.

FROM PORTELA AIRPORT

For general airport information ☎ 218 413 500; www.ana-aeroportas.pt. For flight information ☎ 218 413 700.

The Aerobus (www.carris.pt) leaves from outside Arrivals every 20 minutes (daily 7.45am –8.45pm) making 10 stops in and around the city. Journey time is about 20–30 minutes. Tickets (from the driver) cost €2.85 and are also valid for a day's travel on the Carris public transit network. Scotturb buses run hourly from the airport (daily 7am–10.30pm) direct to Estoril and Cascais. Buy tickets (€7.50) on board. Journey time is about 45 minutes.

Taxis operate a round the clock service from outside the terminal. A ride to the heart of the city should cost €13–€17 (plus €1.50 for luggage and supplements after 10pm and weekends and public holidays). Beware, airport taxis are notorious for overcharging; check that the meter is running or fix a price first, or better still, buy a prepaid taxi voucher from the tourist office in the arrivals hall. Most well-known car-rental companies have desks in the arrivals hall.

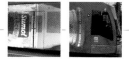

ARRIVING BY TRAIN

International trains and services from Porto, Coimbra and other northern Portuguese towns, plus northern and western suburban services, arrive at Santa Apolónia. Trains from the Algarve and elsewhere in the south arrive at Barreiro. Cais do Sodré has services to and from Estoril and Cascais, and Rossio serves Sintra, Mafra and other suburban and west-coast destinations. Caminhos de Ferro Portugueses is the national rail company (☎ 213 433 748; www.cp.pt).

ARRIVING BY BUS

International and main regional bus services arrive at the Arco do Cego bus station on Avenida João Crisóstomo, north of Marquês de Pombal, in Saldanha. The main national long-distance operator is Rede Expressos (www.rede-expressos.pt), with services from Porto, Faro and other destinations, plus Seville in Spain. International bus services include a daily Eurolines service (☎ 0870 514 3219; www.eurolines.co.uk) from London via Paris. Journey time is 42 hours.

ARRIVING BY CAR

The quickest way to Lisbon from the UK is by car ferry to Bilbao (29–35 hours) or Santander (24 hours). The drive from Santander to Lisbon via Spain and northern Portugal is about 1,000km.

GETTING AROUND

Most buses, trams (*eléctricos*) and lifts (*elevadores*) in Lisbon are run by Carris (☎ 213 613 000; www.carris.pt)—yellow booths around the city provide maps, tickets and information. Buy tickets (interchangeable between buses, trams and lifts) from drivers or kiosks; a pass is the best value (▶ 92). Lisbon also has an efficient four-line Metropolitano (☎ 213 558 457; www. metrolisboa.pt) that runs from 6.30am to 1am. Buy tickets from booths or at machines at the entrance to stations (*estação*). Lisbon's cream or black-and-green taxis are cheap and can be hailed on the street (a green light means a cab is taken) or picked up from ranks such as those at the Baixa-Chiado metro station or Largo de Camões. (▶ 91–92)

ENTRY REQUIREMENTS

EU citizens require a passport or national identity card. US citizens require a passport.

DRIVING IN LISBON

Traffic jams, car theft and the lack of parking make having a car in Lisbon a headache. If you do drive, use a meter or official car park. Improperly parked cars are towed away—contact your local PSP Police station for details of the nearest pound. Holders of old UK pre-EU green licences should carry an International Driving Permit (IDP). Licences issued in the US are accepted.

VISITORS WITH DISABILITIES

Lisbon's busy, narrow and often steep streets can be difficult for visitors with disabilities. Most public buildings and some museums have ramps and other special access. Obtain the Accessible Tourism Guide from the Secretariado Nacional Para a Reabilitação e Integração das Pesoas com Deficiência (✉ Avenida Conde Valbom 63 ☎ 217 929 500; www.snripd.mts. gov.pt) for details.

Living
Lisbon

Lisbon Now

Lisbon's port with the vast suspension bridge which leads to Sintra in the distance

Lisbon is an almost perfect medley of old and new, a glorious remnant of a once-powerful maritime empire mixed with a dynamic, forward-looking city of considerable cultural and social élan. Gradually over the last 25 years this previously moribund capital has become a modern city, catching up with its more prosperous and worldly European rivals with a sustained surge of building, redevelopment and regeneration.

But don't fear, for while shaking off the worst of the past, it has retained much of the quirky and unpretentious charm that makes it such a

NEIGHBOURHOODS

• The heart of Lisbon is the Baixa, a flat grid of streets built after the Great Earthquake in 1755. At its northern limit is the Rossio, the city's main square. East of the Baixa are the hilly and picturesque Alfama and Santa Cruz, which contain the castle and cathedral. West of the Baixa is the old Chiado shopping area, much restored after a fire in 1988, and west of that the Bairro Alto, another hilly district of interesting shops that come alive at night. West again is the more residential Lapa area and the renovated Alcântara docks, another popular nightlife district. Beyond that is Belém, an important historic and cultural area. In the other direction, well to the east of Alfama, is the Parco das Nações, a large waterside suburb developed for the 1998 Expo.

pleasure to visit. Modern office buildings and shopping malls may sprout across the city, muscling in on an atmospheric medley of Moorish and medieval quarters, but in their shadow you will still find streets full of rattling old trams, crumbling mansions, walls of beautiful tiles, quaint mosaic pavements, lovely churches, art nouveau shopfronts, colourful markets and any number of glorious old bars and cafés where the traditional conversational certainties of football, family and religion still hold sway.

Given the speed of change, and its obvious manifestations, it's common to speak of Lisbon as being in the throes of a revolution, as if the change is recent, yet the events that shaped—and continue to shape—the contemporary city have their roots in several key events that have talen place the last four decades.

The first of these was the death in 1970 of the dictator António de Oliveira Salazar, which brought to an end some 35 years of totalitarian rule. In the short term this created political and economic turmoil, but in the longer term it paved the way for the virtually bloodless Portuguese

Strolling through the arcades of Praca do Comercia, Baxia

FACTS & FIGURES

- Lisbon is Europe's most westerly city.
- The city lies almost in the middle of Portugal, 300km (186 miles) from the Algarve to the south and 400km (249 miles) from the Spanish border to the north.
- The population of Lisbon is about 536,000. The figure in 1981 was 807,000. The population of Greater Lisbon is 1.836,000, and that of Lisbon and the Tagus valley 3,327,000—about a third of Portugal's total population.

Above left: *A narrow street in the Alfama District*

Above middle: *The Gare Orient train station at Parques das Nações*

revolution in 1974, and in turn lead to Portugal's entry to the European Union (then known as the European Community) in 1986. Admittance to Europe's high table was a vital turning point, not least because it brought with it a cascade of grants and investment, which—backed by stable government and political reforms—transformed Portugal's economy.

Nowhere was this change more obvious than in Lisbon, where the social and cultural changes wrought by greater prosperity have most made their mark. The city's new cultural swagger was first made manifest on a grand scale in 1994, when Lisbon was named a European City of Culture, and continues today in dazzling new cultural complexes such as the Centro Cultural de

TRAMS

• A great way to see contemporary Lisbon is on one of the city's oldest means of public transport. Trams have been rattling around Lisbon's streets since 1901. Today they run on 72km (45 miles) of track. Take the vintage 28 tram for a memorable sightseeing tour, or the 15 from Praça da Figueira to Bélem for a look at one of the city's modern super-trams.

The Exploding Fountain at Parque das Nações

Belém and its superb Design Museum. It's also apparent in the new funky shops and smart galleries of contemporary art in the Bairro Alto and elsewhere, and in the city's artists and brash young fashion designers who confidently show their work in London, Paris and New York.

Confidence and change are also apparent in the way the city now looks, from the controversial postmodern Amoreiras shopping mall of architect Tomás Taveira to the more carefully integrated Chiado district, which was ravaged by fire in 1988 and sensitively restored over many years under the guidance of architect Álvaro Siza

TILES

• Tiles, or *azulejos*, are found almost everywhere in Lisbon. 'Azulejos' comes from the Arab word *al azulaycha*, meaning 'polished little stone'. The Moors introduced the tile-making art to the Iberian peninsula in the eighth century. Tiles are still used in many contemporary buildings, notably the Cais do Sodré and other metro stations.

LISBOA CARD

• The Lisbon Tourist Card (Cartão-Card Lisboa) gives admittance to over 25 city museums and historic buildings, discounts on over 40 other attractions, and unlimited use of public transport. It is valid for 24 (€12.75), 48 (€21.50) or 72 (€26.55) hours, and is sold at the main tourist office in Praça dos Restauradores, the airport and train stations. Children pay a reduced price for the card.

13

Above left: *A street scene in Barria Alto*

Above middle: *Sun Man by Jorge Viera (1998) in Parque das Nações*

Above right: *The Wall of Water Fountain at Parque das Nações*

Vieira. Lisbon looks out to sea and some of the greatest changes in the city have occured on and around the waterfront. The most obvious is the vast Parque das Nações east of the old city, an area of industrial wasteland that was converted into the site of the Expo '98, the vast trade fair that marked Lisbon's coming of age on the European (and world) stage in 1998. This was the largest urban regeneration in Lisbon's (and Portugal's) history, but it will by no means be the last—a new airport is due to open in 2010, just one of many ongoing projects that continue to transform the city.

Most of Lisbon's citizens have been willing participants in the changes, as you will experince if you visit the dynamic entertainment districts burgeoning around the Alcântara docks west

MODERN CITY

Lisbon's stunning contemporary architecture includes the Armazéns do Chiado—the stylish centrepiece of the Chiado district—and Peter Chermayeff's wondrous Oceanário, the Ponte Vasco da Gama and Álvaro Siza Vieira's extraordinary curved concrete roof for the Pavilhão de Portugal—all architectural marvels at the Parque das Nações.

of the old city. The locals at play reveal a cosmopolitan and sophisticated population that gives the stylish burghers of Paris and Milan, or the clubbing nightowls of London or Ibiza, a hedonistic run for their money. Lisbon's is a vibrant and multicultural population, leavened by immigrants from Portugal's old African and farther-flung colonies, though among these and other of Lisbon's poorer communities you will see the all-too-obvious signs of a city whose transformation still has some way to go. There are some shocking shantytowns on Lisbon's outskirts, along with housing estates and bleak suburban housing, grim compared to other European cities.

But Lisbon's transformation has been dramatic and quick, and in the wrench that has pulled it virtually from the 19th to the 21st century in less than a generation, some people—and places—have inevitably been left behind. At the same time, it is clearly a city on the move, and one where you sense that things can only get better—but also one where you can rest assured that the old charm will never entirely disappear. Come now, and join the party.

DID YOU KNOW?

• Lisbon has more men with moustaches than any other European city.

• The city is on the same latitude as Washington DC, Ibiza, Sicily, San Francisco and Seoul.

• Lisbon has one of Europe's highest traffic accident rates. In one month in 2000 there were 3,500 accidents, leading to 103 deaths.

• Lisbon is 40km (25 miles) from the western edge of continental Europe.

Lisbon Then

A map of 16th-century Lisbon

711 The Moors take control of much of Portugal, including Lisbon.

1139 Afonso Henriques, son of a French count and Castilian princess, declares himself first king of 'Portucale.'

1147 Afonso captures Lisbon from the Moors, after a 17-week siege, with the help of soldiers bound for the Second Crusade.

1195 St. Anthony of Padua is born in Lisbon.

1249 The loss of Faro marks the end of Moorish power in Portugal.

1255 King Afonso III makes Lisbon capital of Portugal, in place of Coimbra.

1385 The Portuguese victory against Castile at the Battle of Aljubarrota secures Portuguese independence for some 200 years.

1580 A crisis in the Portuguese succession allows Philip II of Spain to invade.

1640 The Spanish are overthrown and replaced by the Bragança dynasty of Portuguese kings.

1755 The Great Earthquake destroys two-thirds of Lisbon (► 17, panel).

SEEKING NEW LANDS

In 1419 Henry the Navigator's first square-rigged *barcas* set out in search of a sea route to the Orient. The ship reached Madeira and, eight years later, the Azores.

In 1498 four ships under Vasco da Gama left Lisbon and pioneered a sea route to the East Indies, thus breaking the monopoly of Venetian and Ottoman traders in the East.

Two years later, in 1500, Pedro Álvares Cabral 'discovered' Brazil, whose riches helped to make Portugal the wealthiest country in Europe.

*Lisbon's Great Earthquake,
1st November 1755*

1807 Portugal refuses to join Napoleon's naval blockade of Britain, its ally, and is attacked by a French army.

1810 During the ensuing Peninsular Wars, the Duke of Wellington builds the fortifications known as the Lines of Torres Vedras to protect Lisbon.

1834 The end of the 'War of the Two Brothers' between Dom Pedro IV, emperor of Brazil, and Dom Miguel for Portuguese succession.

1908 King Carlos I is assassinated.

1910 The Portuguese monarchy is over-thrown and replaced by a republic.

1932 Dr António de Oliveira Salazar is made Prime Minister and rules as a dictator until 1968.

1974 The Carnation Revolution of 25 April ends some 40 years of dictatorship.

1986 Portugal joins the European Community (now the European Union).

2002 Euro notes and coins come into circulation, replacing the escudo.

2004 Portugal hosts Euro 2004, the European football championship.

EARTHQUAKE

The Great Earthquake of 1755 began at 9.30am on 1 November–All Saints Day–when many people were at church. The effects of three tremors in ten minutes were made far worse by a tidal wave, 12.5m (41ft) high, and by fires as countless church candles were thrown over. Shock waves were felt as far away as Scotland and Jamaica.

An estimated 60,000 people were killed in Lisbon. Corpses were sunk out at sea to halt epidemics. Taxes were suspended and prices fixed by emergency decree.

Around 9,000 buildings were destroyed but the Marquês de Pombal masterminded the reconstruction of the city.

17

Time to Shop

Vasco de Gama shopping centre in, Parque das Nacoes

Lisbon is not a shopper's haven to compare with London, Paris or New York, but the city does score high for its range of traditional and specialist shops, and in its prices, which, for

SHOPPING CARD

Lisbon's Turismo de Lisboa offers a variety of discount and other passes (► 91), including the Lisboa Shopping Card, which offers up to 20 per cent off in around 200 stores in the Baixa, Chiado, Avenida da Liberdade and other main shopping districts. It comes in two versions, valid for 24 and 72 hours, costing €3.70 and €5.80 respectively (prices valid until March 2005). The passes are available at all Turismo de Lisboa outlets (► 91). For information www.atlx.pt/shopcard.

certain goods, notably shoes and leatherware, are some of the lowest in Western Europe. The city's gentle pace makes it an ideal place for relaxed browsing, but for a more dynamic experience visit one of the city's popular shopping malls.

The main shopping areas are easily defined. The key area has always been the Baixa, whose central grid of streets—unlike those of many modern cities—still retains a wonderful array of traditional and designer stores. Behind the tiny shop fronts, many with lovely art nouveau façades, you'll find everything from Louis Vuitton and La Perla to dusty cobblers and pungent old grocers' stores piled with cheeses, vintage port and other Portuguese staples.

The Bairro Alto district has an altogether more cutting-edge collection of shops, including many small designer fashion outlets, modern furniture showrooms and eccentric stores that reflect the area's chic, bohemian feel. Much the same can be said of the adjacent Chiado, though here the prices are higher and the stores more exclusive. Most big names appear on Avenida da Liberdade with price tags rising the farther north you go.

A street scene in Barrio Alto

Most of the shopping malls are more outlying, though this does nothing to deter Lisboetas, who seem to have taken modern malls to their hearts—the biggest and best are Amoreiras, Colombo and Centro Comercial Vasco da Gama (▶ 72). At the other extreme, Lisbon has plenty of down-to-earth street markets, many worth visiting as much for their local atmosphere as their bargains (▶ panel).

As for Lisbon's best buys, shoes and leatherware are often inexpensive—though styles and sizes may be limited—as are some of the country's traditional foods and wines, not least vintage port, which you'll often find, along with other foodstuffs, at good prices in the supermarkets. Tiles (*azulejos*) and ceramics are also good buys, and make excellent souvenirs to take home, as do wooden craft goods, linens and other textiles. Antiques are never cheap, but you'll find a good selection in and around the Bairro Alto, especially in the shops on Rua de São Bento and Rua Dom Pedro V.

MARKETS

One of Lisbon's most lively shopping experiences is the Feira da Ladra (🔘 Tue and Sat 7am–6.30pm), a flea market at Campo de Santa Clara in the Alfama district. Many stalls sell little more than junk, but there are also stalls with decent antiques, clothes, CDs, handicrafts and more. Best of the food and general markets is the Mercado da Ribeira on Avenida 24 de Julho (🔘 Mon–Sat 5am–7pm), a short walk from Cais do Sodré. Various themed markets take place each Sunday at the Parque das Nações, above the metro station, ranging from stamps and coins, handicrafts, antiques and decorative arts.

Out and About

ORGANIZED TOURS

Details of tour companies can be found in travel agencies, the lobbies of most major hotels and the tourist office in Praça dos Restauradores.

Carris
The public transport company Carris offers four tours of Lisbon and its environs, including the 90-minute Discoveries and Hills Tramway tours (every 30 minutes 9am–6/7pm), plus longer Expresso Oriente and Tagus tours.
✉ Praça do Comércio
☎ 966 298 558

BEACHES

Trains leave Cais do Sodré in Lisbon for Cascais and its three beaches roughly every 20 minutes from 5.30am to 2.30am; journey time 30 minutes.

INFORMATION

MAFRA
Distance 40km (25 miles)
Journey Time 90 minutes
Palácio Nacional de Mafra
☎ 261 810 550
🕐 Wed–Mon 10–5
🚌 Empresa Mafrense buses depart hourly from Largo Martin Moniz, Lisbon
🎫 Moderate

TRAM RIDES AND RIVER TOURS

Trams are an inexpensive way of seeing the city. Tram 28 runs from the Church of São Vicente in the east to the Jardim da Estrela in the west, via the Baixa. Other good routes include the 12 from São Tomé to Largo Martim Moniz and the 15 or

18 (not Sundays) along the waterfront from Praça do Comércio to Belém. In summer there are two tourist tram routes: Circuito Colinas and Circuito Tejo. Ask at the tourist office. Several companies run trips on the River Tagus (April to October). For shorter trips, go to the quays on the Praça do Comércio (► 59). For two-hour cruises (Mar–Oct) contact the tourist office or Cruzeiros no Tejo ☎ 218 820 348/9.

EXCURSIONS
MAFRA

The little town of Mafra is dominated by the Palácio Nacional de Mafra, one of the largest baroque monasteries and palaces in Europe. Begun in 1717, it was built by Dom João V, who had pledged to build a monastery should he and his wife have a child. Bárbara, the future Queen of Spain, was born within a year. Finance for the project was provided by the gold and diamonds of Brazil. The plan was for a monastery of 13 monks—in the end it housed 300. Around 50,000 labourers and 7,000 soldiers worked on the building, a huge folly of 880 rooms. Today you can visit the rather chilly church and rooms.

SINTRA

Sintra is a town of sumptuous royal palaces and beautiful scenery. It is not a single sight, however, and can be disorienting. You will need to use taxis or a car to move between sights, or join an organized tour, as buses are irregular.

In Sintra-Vila (the town itself) the main thing to see is the Palácio Nacional, begun by Dom João I in the 15th century and used as a royal palace until the end of the 19th century. Just south of Sintra-Vila lies the Castelo dos Mouros, a Moorish castle begun in the 8th century. The views from its rocky pinnacles are magnificent. Further south, around 3km (1.8 miles) from Sintra-Vila, lies another royal palace, the Palácio da Pena, a wonderfully pretentious monument built in the 19th century. A madcap medieval pastiche, its exterior is all battlements and towers. Its park and gardens are delightful, and the views from its terraces sublime. For still better panoramas, try the nearby Cruz Alta (529m/1,735ft), the highest point in the Serra de Sintra hills.

Palácio de Monserrate is a pastoral idyll 4km (2.5 miles) west of Sintra. Another must is the recently restored Quinta da Regaleira, just to the east of Sintra. It is one of the finest examples of late 19th-century revivalist art, with its masonic 'well of initiation', gargoyles, mythological grottos and neo-Manueline palace and chapel.

INFORMATION

SINTRA
Distance 25km (16 miles)
Journey Time 45 minutes by train
🚊 From Lisbon's Estação Rossio, every 20 minutes
🛈 Praça da República 23 (☎ 219 231 157; www.cm-sintra.pt)
Palácio Nacional da Vila de Sintra
✉ Largo da Rainha D Amélia
☎ 219 106 840
🕐 Tue–Thu 10–5.30
💶 Moderate
Castelo dos Mouros
✉ Calçada dos Clérigos
🕐 Jun–end Sep daily 9–8; Oct–end Mar daily 9–7 💶 Moderate
Palácio Nacional da Pena
✉ Estrada da Pena
☎ 219 105 340
🕐 Palace mid-Jun to mid-Sep Tue–Sun 10–7; rest of year 10–5. Park daily 💶 Expensive
Palácio de Monserrate
✉ Estrada de Monserrate
☎ 219 247 200
🕐 Gardens only: daily 9–8 (6/7 in winter) 💶 Free
Quinta da Regaleira
✉ Quinta da Regaleira
☎ 219 106 650
🕐 Jun–end Sep 10–5; Oct, Feb–end May 10–6.30; Jan, Dec 10–5.30
💶 Expensive

Right: *Pena Palace in Sintra*
Left: *Convento Palacio in Mafra*

Walks

INFORMATION

Distance 3.5km (2 miles)
Time 2–3 hours
Start point ★ Praça dos Restauradores
✚ H7; all
Ⓜ Restauradores
End point Baixa
✚ J8; bIII
Ⓜ Baixa–Chiado

BAIXA, CASTELO AND ALFAMA

Head south from Praça dos Restauradores. Note the lovely old façade of the Rossio railway station on your right (Praça João da Câmara). Walk down the Rossio, Lisbon's main square, and then pick up Rua Augusta, a pedestrianized street through the Baixa. At the end look at the Praça do Comércio. Then go back into the Baixa and turn right on to Rua da Conceição, crossing Largo da Madalena. Climb to the Sé (cathedral). Then follow the street uphill to the left of the cathedral.

Continue to Santa Luzia and its viewpoint (*miradouro*). Cross the road to see the Museu das Artes Decorativas (Decorative Arts Museum). As you leave the museum, turn right (back the way you came) and take the first right (Travessa de Santa Luzia) and continue uphill (bearing right), following the yellow signs to the Castelo de São Jorge. Walk the length of the walkway under the castle walls, emerging through a green iron gate into Largo do Menino de Deus (down to your left). Turn left into the shabby square and find Rua da Santa Marinha at its top (north) side. Follow to São Vicente de Fora church. Take the street to the left of the church into Campo de Santa Clara. Walk to the small garden and palm trees, then drop right to come around behind the church of Santa Engrácia. With your back to the façade go left down past the brown-tiled house ahead. Turn right on to Rua dos Remédios at the bottom.

Detour south to visit the Museu Nacional Militar, or turn right on to Rua São Estêvão and then turn left to pick up the atmospheric Rua São Miguel. Return to the cathedral on Rua de São João de Praça, and go back to the Baixa.

Cascading water from a fountain in the Praca do Rossio

CHIADO SHOPPING STREETS

This is not a long walk, but it can be extended to take in the streets of the Bairro Alto to the north and west. However, the character of the two adjoining districts is very different, and in the Bairro Alto—where the streets are like a maze—it is difficult to follow any set itinerary.

Begin in the Rossio and take the pedestrianized Rua do Carmo uphill. On your left you pass the Elevador de Santa Justa, built in 1902 and often wrongly attributed to Gustave Eiffel (it was designed by Raul Mésnier, one of his pupils).

Turn right into Rua Garrett, the Chiado's most prestigious street. Walk to the top and note the statue of poet Fernando Pessoa and the splendid old Café A Brasileira on its right. A few doors to the right on the same side of the street is the equally revered Pastelaria Benard.

Turn back down Rua Garrett a few steps and look into the Igreja dos Mártires, a church erected over a 12th-century burial ground and camp of the Crusaders during the siege of Lisbon. Take Rua Serpa Pinto to the right of the church and walk down past the Teatro São Carlos and the hospital.

Visit the Museu do Chiado, then continue to the bottom of the street. Turn right and then right again to double back up to Rua Garrett. Turn left into the square, right up Rua da Misericórdia, and take the first right at Largo da Trindade. Then turn right and left to follow Rua da Trindade to the shady Largo do Carmo.

Visit the ruined Carmo church and museum. Then follow Rua da Oliveira northeast and turn right down the steps, noticing the narrow view of the Baixa and Castelo. Follow the steps down past the station and cross Rua 1 de Dezembro to return to the Rossio.

INFORMATION

Distance 2km (1.2 miles)
Time 2 hours with visits
Start/end point
★ Rossio
🚇 H8; bIII
Ⓡ Rossio

A statue of poet Fernando Pessoa outside a Brasileira café in Rue Garrett

23

Lisbon by Night

Above left: *The Barrio Alto after dark*

Above right: *Sé cathedral lit-up at night*

Not so long ago, nightlife in Lisbon consisted of little more than a handful of old bars, restaurants and the occasional live enter-tainment in the shape of fado, the country's traditional music (▶ 84). But as the rest of the city has changed, so has its nightlife, and today Lisbon has a huge selection of cutting-edge bars and state-of-the-art discos, as well as one of Europe's most dynamic clubbing scenes.

WHERE TO PARTY

Much of the action takes place on the Bairro Alto, whose many sleek bars, clubs and lounges heave with up to 50,000 revellers nightly on the busiest evenings of the week. As the night wears on, many of these revellers drift west to the clubs on Avenida 24 de Julho, or to the Alcântara, a rejuvenated docks area whose waterfront—especially the Doca de Santo Amaro—has been almost entirely given over to late-opening, warehouse-style bars and clubs. Revellers have also moved east, to the even newer nightlife districts of the Parque das Nações and Santa Apolónia waterfront.

SOMETHING A LITTLE MORE SEDATE

City nightlife need not just be a frantic round of clubs. There are occasional opera and other classical music concerts, many staged outdoors when the weather allows. And on a summer evening, of course, nightlife need consist of no more than a relaxing meal under the stars, a quiet drink in an atmospheric bar or a balmy evening stroll through some of the old city's more sedate streets.

LISBON's
top 25 sights

The sights are shown on the maps on the inside front cover and inside back cover, numbered **1**–**25** across the city

Torre de Belém

- The Torre de Belém was declared a World Heritage Site by the United Nations in 1983

INFORMATION

- B10
- Avenida de Brasília
- 213 620 034
- Tue–Sun 10–5. Closed Mon and public hols
- 27, 28, 29, 43, 49, 51; tram 15
- Belem (Cascais line) from Cais do Sodré
- Very poor
- Moderate
- Museu de Marinha (► 27), Museu Nacional de Arqueologia (► 28), Padrão dos Descobrimentos (► 29), Mosteiro dos Jerónimos (► 30), Museu Nacional dos Coches (► 31)

Delicate stonework on the Torre de Belém

Few buildings are as charming or evocative as the Torre de Belém, a capricious architectural confection of towers, turrets and battlements, whose tawny-coloured ramparts are washed by the River Tagus on three sides.

National landmark Lisbon's Belém tower is not only a masterpiece of Renaissance and Manueline architecture, but also one of Portugal's most potent national symbols. A monument to the country's maritime triumphs across the centuries, it was built between 1515 and 1520 by Francisco de Arruda, a Portuguese architect who had previously worked on a variety of military projects in Morocco. His travels in North Africa made a lasting impression on him, and this is reflected in the use of a wide range of Moorish motifs on the tower. Chief of these are the little domes crowning the battlements, and the jutting corner sentry boxes, which are combined with arcaded windows and delicate Venetian-style loggias.

Changing roles Once the tower stood proudly out in the river, acting as a defensive bastion guarding the Restelo, or harbour, from pirates. Today the Tagus's ever-changing course has left it stranded on the shore. Close to, you can make out the cross motif adorning every battlement. This was the symbol of the Order of Christ, the successor to the Knights Templar in Portugal. A jutting bastion leads to a small internal cloister, below which are rudimentary storerooms and dungeons (the tower served as a prison from 1580 to 1828). The breezy second-storey terrace —which gives good views—features an intricately carved statue of the Madonna (Our Lady of the Safe Homecoming). Steps lead up to the top of the tower for more views.

Museu de Marinha

Lisbon's excellent maritime museum is irresistible, even if you don't admire boats. It is one of the most important of its kind in Europe, and fully captures the splendour of Portugal's long and distinguished history of seafaring.

Seafaring nation It seems only right that Lisbon's maritime museum should be in Belém, for it was from the sheltered harbour nearby that many of the great Portuguese explorers embarked on their voyages of discovery. Today the museum occupies both the west wing of the Mosteiro dos Jerónimos, and part of the nearby Galeotas Pavilion. The former contains to a collection of model boats and other maritime ephemera, the latter full-size craft, planes and several impressive royal barges. There is also a children's museum, the Museu das Crianças.

Maritime History The bulk of the museum's more venerable exhibits were provided by a private bequest in 1948. So many items were lost or destroyed in the 1755 earthquake that it was not easy to find early artefacts for the museum. Much of the collection proceeds chronologically, from the era of the Great Discoveries onwards. The oldest exhibit is a wooden figure representing the Archangel Raphael, which accompanied Vasco da Gama on his pioneering voyage to the Indies in 1497. From the 19th century comes the ornate splendour of royal yachts, including a reconstruction of a sumptuous cabin from the *Amélia*, built for Carlos I. There is also a section devoted to the Orient and other maritime memorabilia. Don't miss the outstanding Museu de Centro Cultural de Belém nearby (➤ 52, panel).

HIGHLIGHTS

- State barges (Pavilhão das Galeotas)
- Model boats
- Statue of Archangel Raphael
- Cabins of the *Amélia*
- Paintings
- Prows
- Maps

INFORMATION

www.museumarinha.pt
- B9
- Praça do Império
- 213 620 019
- Apr–end Sep Tue–Sun 10–6; Oct–end Mar Tue–Sun 10–5. Closed public hols
- 27, 28, 29, 43, 49, 51; tram 15
- Belém (Cascais line) from Cais do Sodré
- Very good
- Moderate
- Museu Nacional de Arqueologia (➤ 28), Mosteiro dos Jerónimos (➤ 30), Padrão dos Descobrimentos (➤ 29), Torre de Belém (➤ 26)
- Entrance at western end of the Mosteiro dos Jerónimos

Wooden figure of the Archangel Raphael

27

Museu Nacional de Arqueologia

HIGHLIGHTS

- Funerary monuments
- Granite boars
- Early pottery
- Roman mosaics
- Sarcophagi
- Jewellery
- Treasury

INFORMATION

www.mnarqueologia-
ipmuseus.pt

⊞ C9

✉ Praça do Império

☎ 213 620 000/213 620 022

🕐 Wed–Sun 10–6, Tue 2–6.
Closed public hols

🚌 14, 17, 27, 28, 29, 43, 49,
51; tram 15, 16, 17

🚊 Belém (Cascais line) from
Cais do Sodré

♿ Good

💷 Moderate

🔄 Museu de Marinha
(➤ 27), Torre de Belém
(➤ 26), Padrão dos
Descobrimentos (➤ 29),
Mosteiro dos Jerónimos
(➤ 30), Museu Nacional
dos Coches (➤ 31)

❓ Entrance mid-way along
the main façade of the
Mosteiro dos Jerónimos

You might consider this rambling archaeological museum a little threadbare in places, but there are plenty of fascinating artefacts from widely differing epochs of Portuguese history to make a visit worthwhile.

Look back in time Since its foundation in 1893, the National Archaeology Museum has been in the east wing of the Mosteiro dos Jerónimos, making it easy to visit in conjunction with the monastery church and the Museu de Marinha in the adjoining west wing. The collection includes a mixture of archaeological and ethnographical items, including folk objects and religious artefacts illustrating Portugal's broader history, from the Neolithic (the late Stone Age) onwards. Earthenware pottery and funerary headstones make up the bulk of the Neolithic remains, while the Iron Age section includes the strange granite monoliths known as *berrões*, or boars, which are common in many parts of northeast Portugal.

Highlights The museum becomes really enthralling in the Roman section, which has mosaics, statues and embellished sarcophagi gathered from sites across Portugal. These are some of the collection's most eye-catching sights. Look out in particular for the bronze figurine representing Fortune, and the Quadriga, a sculptural group of four horses pulling a chariot. Other sections are devoted to African exhibits, Egyptian pieces in particular, and to items garnered from Portugal's overseas empire or brought back by Portuguese traders. Some of the museum's loveliest exhibits are to be found in the treasury, where you can see an amazing range of Celtic earrings, bracelets, rings and other intricately worked jewellery.

*Bronze figurine of
Fortune, 1st century AD*

Padrão dos Descobrimentos

It must have taken courage to impose a vast modern monument on an area as historical as Belém, but this huge white waterfront edifice provides a dramatic and dignified counterpart to the venerable Torre de Belém nearby.

Maritime pride The Monument to the Discoveries was erected in 1960 during the Salazar dictatorship. It marked the 500th anniversary of the death of Henry the Navigator, the prince who laid the foundation of Portugal's wide-reaching empire through his energetic backing of projects such as a maritime school in the Algarve. The monument has been criticised for its vaguely fascist design and obviously nationalist intent, but it is nonetheless an architectural triumph, imposing itself on the Belém waterfront. Its jutting triangular pediment represents the prow of a ship, while the trio of curving forms above symbolises billowing sails. Rising over these is a redoubtable blockhouse tower, reaching some 52m above the quayside.

Figures The monument's rigid lines are softened by a group of sculpted figures crowded on the pediment's sloping prow. Behind Henry, who holds a ship in his hands, stands Manuel I, the king who reigned from 1495 to 1521, during the height of Portugal's voyages of discovery. He is shown holding an armillary sphere, one of his regal symbols. Other characters include Luís de Camões (▶ 75), one of Portugal's most famous poets, who is depicted holding verses. A lift runs to the top of the monument, from where you can look down on a mosaic map depicting the voyages of discovery.

HIGHLIGHTS

- Henry the Navigator
- Views from balcony
- Mosaic map

INFORMATION

- 🔢 C10
- ✉️ Avenida de Brasília
- ☎️ 213 031 950
- 🕐 Jun–end Sep Tue–Sun 9–6.30; Oct–end May Tue–Sun 9–5. Closed public hols
- 🚌 27, 28, 43, 49; tram 15
- 🚆 Belém (Cascais line) from Cais do Sodré
- ♿ Good
- 💰 Moderate
- ↔️ Museu de Arqueologia (▶ 28), Mosteiro dos Jerónimos (▶ 30), Museu Nacional dos Coches (▶ 31)

Top: *Mosaic map.*
Below: *Henry leads pediment statues*

Mosteiro dos Jerónimos

DID YOU KNOW?

- The monastery was declared a World Heritage Site by the United Nations in 1983

HIGHLIGHTS

- South door
- West door
- Fan vaulting
- Nave
- Monument to Vasco da Gama
- Transept star vaulting
- Choir stalls

INFORMATION

www.mosteirojeronimos.pt

➕ C9

✉ Praça do Império

☎ 213 620 034

🕐 May–end Sep Tue–Sun 10–6.30; Oct–end Apr Tue–Sun 10–5

🚌 27, 28, 29, 43, 49, 51; tram 15

🚊 Belém (Cascais line) from Cais do Sodré

♿ Poor

💶 Moderate

🔁 Museu Nacional de Arqueologia (► 28), Museu de Marinha (► 27), Padrão dos Descobrimentos (► 29), Museu Nacional dos Coches (► 31)

❓ Tram 15 stops outside the monastery. The return stop is 150m east, opposite Casa dos Pastéis

There are no greater buildings in Lisbon than those of the Mosteiro dos Jerónimos, a glorious monastic complex whose carved stonework and magnificent cloisters rival Europe's finest Gothic and Renaissance work.

Praising the explorers The present monastery is built over the site of a small chapel raised by Henry the Navigator in 1460 to provide spiritual solace to the many seafarers who embarked on voyages of discovery from Belém. The new church was begun by Manuel I in 1502 to celebrate Vasco da Gama's successful voyage to the Indies, da Gama having held a vigil in Henry's chapel prior to his 1497 expedition. Some 50 years were to elapse before the building was completed, and during this time several architects worked on the project, hence the Gothic, Manueline and Renaissance mixture of the church's artistic and architectural styles.

Treasures The monastery's treasures begin with the magnificent south door, whose wealth of decoration focuses on the figure of Henry the Navigator (above the arch), and the contrasting west door, where the protagonists are Manuel I, his wife, Dona Maria, and the pair's respective patron saints. Inside are soaring aisles and a vast, breathtaking array of carved stone, reaching a climax in the huge sweep of fan vaulting over the nave. Take time to search out da Gama's tomb, located beneath a gallery near the church's entrance, and then make for the adjoining cloisters, one of Portugal's great architectural set-pieces. The two-storey ensemble, and the lower tier in particular, is a feast of outstanding carving, the pillars and vaults embellished with a wealth of intricately sculpted stone, whose delicacy belies its strength and weight.

Museu Nacional dos Coches

It is difficult to imagine that a coach museum could be one of Lisbon's most visited sights until you go for yourself and see the sheer splendour of its beautifully embellished coaches and carriages.

Travel in style Lisbon's National Coach Museum is one of the best collections of its type in the world. For the Portuguese royalty and aristocracy, coaches and carriages were never merely modes of transport, but were used to proclaim the wealth and taste of their owners. As a result many were painted, gilded and decorated to a magnificent degree, particularly those used for state or ceremonial occasions. The museum, founded by Queen Amélia in 1904, is in the former riding academy and stables of the Palácio do Belém, a royal palace begun around 1726 by Dom João V. Today the palace proper, which is not open to visitors, is the official residence of the Portuguese president.

Rich collection Three of the museum's most splendid coaches are those built in 1716 for the Marquês de Frontes, Portugal's ambassador to Pope Clement XI and the Holy See. Constructed in Italy, the coaches are decorated with allegorical scenes representing Portuguese military and maritime triumphs. Other highlights include many cabs, prams and sedans; the royal carriage of Dom José I; a miniature carriage built for King Carlos I as a child; and the berlin made for Dona Maria I for the opening of the Basílica da Estrela. If the museum has a fault it is that there are just too many coaches, the endless repetition dulling the wonderful impression created by the first displays.

HIGHLIGHTS

- Painted ceiling vaults
- Coaches of the Marquês de Frontes
- Dom João V's state coach
- Dom José I's state coach
- King Carlo I's miniature carriage
- Dona Maria I's royal carriage

Detail on coach

INFORMATION

www.museudoscoches-ipmuseus.pt

C9

Praça Afonso de Albuquerque

213 610 850

Tue–Sun 10–6 (last entry 5.30). Closed public hols

14, 27, 28, 29, 43, 49, 51; tram 15

Belém (Cascais line) from Cais do Sodré

Poor Moderate

Mosteiro dos Jerónimos (► 30)

31

Palácio dos Marquêses de Fronteira

HIGHLIGHTS

- Battle Room
- Delft, or Dining, Room
- Gallery of Arts (tiled terrace)
- Chapel
- Gardens
- Doze de Inglaterra
- Statues of the Nine Muses
- Statues of Portugal's first 15 kings

INFORMATION

✚ E5

✉ Largo de São Domingos de Benfica 1

☎ 217 782 023

🕐 Palace guided tours Jun–end Sep Mon–Sat 10.30, 11, 11.30 and noon; Oct–end May Mon–Sat 11 and noon

🚇 Sete Rios

🚌 72

♿ Poor

💶 Gardens moderate. Palace and gardens expensive. Admission more expensive on Sat

❓ Gardens not included in tour when it is raining. Opening times change regularly; call for latest details. The palace can only be visited on an official tour at the specified times. English tours available

Top: *Picture tiles in the gardens of the Fronteira Palace*

Even if you are usually a little lazy when it comes to trekking out to the suburbs of a city, the beautiful Italianate gardens and captivating tiles make the journey to the Fronteira Palace more than worthwhile.

Isolated beauty A train or metro ride from the Rossio drops you close to the Fronteira Palace in an area of somewhat moribund modern housing and half-finished roads. The palace and its gardens, an oasis of beauty in this wasteland, were founded in 1670 as a hunting lodge by João Mascarenhas, the first Marquês de Fronteira. The palace is still privately owned, but guided tours conduct you around some half-dozen rooms, notably the Battle Room, whose tiled decoration depicts scenes from the War of Restoration. This campaign brought to an end 60 years of Spanish domination in Portugal between 1581 and 1640. Fronteira was a general, and played a prominent part in the war.

Gardens The palace's Italianate gardens, full of fountains, topiary terraces, little lakes and a dense green web of clipped hedging, are a delight, not least because of the *azulejos*, or tiles, which decorate virtually every suitable surface. You will already have seen a wide variety of tiles in the palace, including some of the first Delft tiles imported into Portugal (in the 17th century). In the gardens, there are benches, walls and ornamental pools swathed with tiles depicting all manner of subjects—the months of the year, the planets, the signs of the zodiac and many more. The most eye-catching are the life-size depictions of the Doze de Inglaterra, 12 gallant horsemen who, according to the legend, sailed to England to fight for the honour of 12 damsels in distress.

Museu Nacional de Arte Antiga

Lisbon may have few internationally acclaimed galleries, but in this wonderful museum—not to mention the Gulbenkian Museum—the city has a gallery that stands up to comparison with almost any throughout Europe.

Collection The National Museum of Ancient Art contains one of Portugal's finest art collections, and ranks second only to the Gulbenkian among Lisbon's galleries and museums. The collection of paintings shows the development of Portuguese art from about the 11th century onwards, and also includes work by several of Europe's greatest artists. There is a wealth of decorative art and silverware, notably Italian ceramics, ecclesiastical vestments, Flemish tapestries, and a monstrance from the Mosteiro (► 30) in Belém, reputedly made from the first gold brought back from the Indies by Vasco da Gama. Also worth seeing are a decorated chapel, preserved from a convent previously on the site, and the Namban screens, which depict the arrival of the Portuguese in Japan in 1543.

Adoration The museum's most famous painting by far is an altarpiece, the *Painéis de São Vicente de Fora*, or *Adoration of St. Vincent*, thought to be painted by Nuno Gonçalves between 1465 and 1470. The work was discovered only in 1882, dirty and dismembered in a defunct Lisbon church. Its six panels portray around 60 figures paying homage to St. Vincent, Lisbon's patron saint, who is depicted twice. Other treasures include works by Grão Vasco, Frei Carlos Memling, Holbein, Dürer, Raphael and Velázquez.

HIGHLIGHTS

- *Adoration of St. Vincent*, Nuno Gonçalves
- Cook Triptych, Grão Vasco
- *Annunciation*, Frei Carlos
- *Temptation of St. Antony*, Hieronymus Bosch
- *Madonna and Child*, Memling
- *St Jerome*, Albrecht Dürer
- *St Augustine*, Piero della Francesca
- French silver tableware
- Japanese Namban screens

INFORMATION

www.mnarteantiga-ipmuseus.pt

- G9
- Rua das Janelas Verdes-Jardim 9 de Abril
- 213 912 800
- Wed–Sun 10–6, Tue 2–6
- Small bar and restaurant
- 27, 40, 49, 51, 60; tram 15, 18, 25
- Santos (Cascais line)
- Very good: lift, small steps
- Moderate
- Basílica da Estrela (► 34)

Top: The Adoration of St. Vincent. Left: statue of St Trinity

33

Basílica da Estrela

INFORMATION

- G8
- Largo da Estrela
- 213 960 915
- Daily 8–1, 3–8
- Rato
- 20, 22, 38; tram 25, 28
- Poor
- Free
- Museu Nacional de Arte Antiga (▶ 33)

A massive dome crowns the Basílica

The chill austerity of neo-classical architecture is not to everyone's taste, but it is difficult to remain unaffected by the sheer scale of a building like the Estrela basilica—not to mention the sweeping views from its dome.

Offering Like the Palácio de Fronteira, the Basílica da Estrela lies some way from the heart of the city—2km to the west of the Bairro Alto—but it is more than worth the effort required to see it. You will be doubly rewarded if you combine a trip here with a visit to the Jardim de Estrela (Jardim Guerra Junqueiro), one of the city's most beautiful gardens (▶ 58). The basilica, a monumental white edifice, was founded by Dona Maria I in 1779 as a votive offering for the birth of a son. Begun in the same year, it is a neo-classical masterpiece, and one of Lisbon's most imposing 18th-century buildings.

Impressive The church's architects, Mateus Vicente and Reinaldo Manuel, were influenced by the convent at Mafra (▶ 20), a building whose main attribute is size. Size is also the basilica's defining feature, the austere interior a cavernous expanse of marble. To the left of the high altar lies the tomb of Dona Maria I, who died in Brazil in 1816 and whose body was returned to Portugal for burial six years later. Unlike male scions of the Bragança royal dynasty, who were embalmed for posterity, Maria was simply adorned with herbs and enclosed in three tight-closing coffins, one inside the other. It is said that when these were opened to transfer the body back to Portugal, two ladies-in-waiting assisting in the ceremony fainted at the stench from the putrefied corpse.

Museu Calouste Gulbenkian

If given the job of putting together an art gallery with unlimited funds, you would come up with something close to the Gulbenkian. Its range is complete, from ancient to modern, famous to obscure and from east to west.

Bequest to the nation The Gulbenkian is Portugal's single greatest museum. Run by the Fundação Calouste Gulbenkian, it is one of the countless artistic and cultural initiatives financed by a bequest from Calouste Gulbenkian (1869–1955), an Armenian oil magnate. It was built between 1964 and 1969 by architects Alberto Passoal, Pedro Cid and Ruy Athouguia. Gulbenkian's extensive private art collection makes up the bulk of the museum's collection, which is divided into two sections: The first deals with ancient and Oriental exhibits, the second with European art and artefacts.

Stunning collection The European section embraces paintings, sculptures and the decorative arts. Exhibits are arranged chronologically and, wherever possible, according to school and nationality. The paintings include works by Manet, Degas, Renoir, Van Dyck, Frans Hals, Ghirlandaio, Turner and Gainsborough. Pride of place goes to Rembrandt's *Alexander the Great* and captivating *Portrait of an Old Man*. Among the wealth of tapestries, furniture, silverware and other beautiful artefacts, look out in particular for the stunning jewellery by René Lalique (in a reverentially darkened room at the end of the gallery). In the ancient and Oriental sections the highlights include Chinese porcelain, Japanese lacquer work and silk and wool carpets. End your visit with a walk in the foundation's lovely gardens. There is also a tasteful café in the museum basement.

HIGHLIGHTS

- Rembrandt paintings
- Islamic ceramics
- Lalique jewellery and glass
- Carpets
- French ivory diptychs

Rembrandt's Portrait of an Old Man *Top: Famille Rose porcelain*

INFORMATION

- **www**.gulbenkian.pt
- G5
- Avenida de Berna 45
- 217 823 461
- Tue 2–6, Wed–Sun 10–6. Closed public hols
- Café
- São Sebastião/Praça de Espanha
- 16, 26, 31, 46, 56
- Rego
- Excellent
- Expensive. Free on Sun
- Centro de Arte Moderna (▶ 36)
- Downhill from metro, turn right after 300m

35

11

Centro de Arte Moderna

HIGHLIGHTS

- Henry Moore
- Amadeu de Souza-Cardoso
- Guilherme Santa Rita
- Paula Rego
- João Cutileiro
- Vieira da Silva
- Julio Pomar
- Costa Pinheiro

INFORMATION

www.gulbenkian.pt

- G5
- Rua Dr Nicolau de Bettencourt
- 217 823 474
- Tue–Sun 10–5.30. Closed public hols.
- São Sebastião/Praça de Espanha
- 16, 26, 31, 46, 56
- Rego
- Good
- Moderate or joint ticket with Gulbenkian Museum (expensive). Free on Sun
- Museu Calouste Gulbenkian (➤ 35)

Names of modern Portuguese artists will be unfamiliar to most people, but there's no better place to become acquainted with their work than this state-of-the-art gallery sponsored by the Calouste Gulbenkian Foundation.

Parkland gem Lisbon's Centre for Modern Art lies just around the corner from the better-known Museu Calouste Gulbenkian. Like its near neighbour, it was made possible by the legacy of Calouste Gulbenkian, the Armenian oil magnate, who left his art collection and a slice of his fortune to Portugal. The art centre is set in the same park, and is on display in a beautiful modern building designed by the British architect Sir Leslie Martin and opened in 1983. The museum's airy exhibition space—all clean lines and abundant greenery—is a pleasure in itself, admirably complementing a collection of over 10,000 works of art.

National collection The parkland surrounding the museum is scattered with sculptures, of which the most notable is the *Reclining Woman* by Henry Moore, close to the main entrance. Inside, the gallery's eminent Portuguese painters include Amadeu de Souza-Cardoso and Guilherme Santa Rita, both of whom were influenced by the Italian Futurists. In acknowledging the work of foreign painters, the pair were typical of Portuguese artists, most of whom worked or studied abroad. By following such foreign styles and not establishing their own movement few artists from Portugal are said to have strongly influenced the evolution of modern art. Almada Negreiros is credited as founder of Portuguese modernism, and others who have become known outside Portugal include Paula Rego, João Cutileiro, Vieira da Silva, Julio Pomar and Costa Pinheiro.

Bairro Alto

Traditionally the bohemian haunt of students, artists and writers, the narrow cobbled streets of the Bairro Alto, home of the traditional fado singing, should not be missed on any visit to the city.

Nightlife The Bairro Alto, or Upper Town, is one of Lisbon's liveliest and most distinctive quarters, and one of the five loosely defined neighbourhoods that make up the heart of the old city. Traditionally a working-class area, it was hardly damaged by the 1755 earthquake, and rises in a close-knit grid of 16th-century streets up the steep slopes west of the Chiado and Baixa districts. During the day its quiet corners are filled with the sort of evocative scenes you find all over Lisbon—washing strung from the windows and grubby children playing in the streets. As night falls, by contrast, the restaurants and bars open and by 10pm the strains of fado (▶ 84) can be heard as the area becomes the principal focus of Lisbon's nightlife.

Sights Exploring the Bairro's streets is an activity worth pursuing for its own sake, but some sights deserve special attention. These include the Elevador de Santa Justa, a clanking old elevator built in 1902, and the Elevador da Glória, a funicular built in 1885. Both save you a lot of climbing by carrying you up from the Baixa district below. Other sights are the Solar do Vinho do Porto, run by the Port Wine Institute (▶ 80, panel) and the Igreja de São Roque (▶ 38). The Miradouro de São Pedro de Alcântara has some fine views over the city (▶ 55).

HIGHLIGHTS

- Elevador de Santa Justa
- Elevador da Glória
- Solar do Vinho do Porto
- Igreja de São Roque
- Miradouro de São Pedro de Alcântara (▶ 55)
- Rua de Atalaia (shopping)
- Rua do Diário de Notícias (shopping)

INFORMATION

- H7–H8; aIl–aIll
- Streets enclosed by Rua da Boa Vista, Rua da Misericórdia, Rua do Século and Rua Dom Pedro V
- Many bars and cafés
- Baixa-Chiado or Restauradores/ Elevador da Glória
- Tram 28
- Very poor
- Igreja de São Roque (▶ 38), Chiado (▶ 39), Museu Arqueológico do Carmo (▶ 40)

Left: *The Elevador de Santa Justa takes you up to Chiado and the Bairro Alto beyond*

37

Igreja de São Roque

Asked to highlight the most extravagant piece of decorative folly in Lisbon, you would have no hesitation in plumping for the Igreja de São Roque, and in particular its chapels, which groan under the weight of gold, gilt, marble and other precious materials.

HIGHLIGHTS

- Painted wooden ceiling
- Capela de São Roque
- Tile decoration
- Capela de São João Baptista
- Mosaics

INFORMATION

- ✚ H8; all
- ✉ Largo Trindade Coelho
- ☎ 213 235 381
- 🕓 Museum: Tue–Sun 10–5. Closed public hols. Church daily 8.30–6
- Ⓜ Baixa-Chiado
- 🚌 58, 100
- ♿ Poor
- 🎫 Church free. Museum inexpensive; free on Sun and public hols
- ⟷ Bairro Alto (➤ 37), Chiado (➤ 39), Museu Arqueológico do Carmo (➤ 40)

Lavish interior Little in the plain façade of this church prepares you for the decorative splendour within. Commissioned by the Jesuits in the 16th century, the building of 1565 was the work of Filippo Terzi, also responsible for the church of São Vicente across the city. His original façade fell victim to the 1755 earthquake, but not the interior, which was saved, according to popular belief, by the personal intervention of St. Roch (São Roque). Inside, the trompe l'œil painting on the ceiling is a triumph, while each of the eight chapels lining the nave is a decorative masterpiece. The third on the right, the Capela de São Roque, has some of the finest *azulejos* (tiles) in the city, the work of Francisco de Matos in 1584, his only known commission.

Chapel The fourth chapel on the left, the Capela de São João Baptista, though less immediately impressive, has been called the most expensive chapel for its size ever built. Commissioned in 1742 by João V, it was designed by Vanvitelli, the papal architect, and built in Rome. There it was blessed by Pope Benedict XIV before being shipped to Lisbon, where its ensemble of precious materials—ivory, amethyst, porphyry and Carrara marble among others—was reassembled. Note the chapel's 'paintings', which are not paintings but extra-ordinarily detailed mosaics. Beside the church is the Museu de Arte Sacra, with a rich collection of paintings, embroidery and ecclesiastical plates.

Baroque extravagance in São Roque's Capela de Nossa Sra da Assumpta

Chiado

Despite its damage by fire in 1988, today the Chiado thrives. Modern boutiques and department stores, hidden behind beautifully restored façades, sit harmoniously beside Lisbon's oldest shops and wood-panelled cafés.

District The Chiado is one of the five loosely defined districts that make up the heart of old Lisbon. Named after the poet António Ribeiro who was nicknamed O Chiado, meaning 'Squeaky', it lies just alongside the Baixa, spreading across the first of the slopes that rise westwards to the Bairro Alto. Known primarily as a shopping district, it embraces not only the main Largo do Chiado, but also a range of streets around the Rua Garrett and Rua do Carmo. Affluent and fashionable, its streets contain many luxury shops and fine old cafés, notably A Brasileira in Rua Garrett. Also here are the Teatro São Carlos opera house and the Igreja dos Mártires, the latter built over the site of a Crusader burial ground and encampment.

Destruction On 25 August 1988 the Chiado achieved unwanted fame when it was ravaged by fire. The conflagration is thought to have started in a store on Rua do Carmo, and devastated four blocks of the district before being brought under control. Some 2,000 people lost their jobs, and many old buildings were gutted, including the famous Ferrari coffee-house and Grandella department store. In the disaster's aftermath the Mayor of Lisbon entrusted the reconstruction of the area to Alvaro Siza Vieira, a celebrated Portuguese architect, who resolved to rebuild the district to a classical plan in keeping with the existing structures. Much of the rebuilding and restoration has now been successfully completed.

HIGHLIGHTS

- Rua Garrett
- Teatro de São Carlos
- Igreja dos Mártires
- Museu Arqueológico do Carmo (➤ 38)
- Café A Brasileira (➤ 69)
- Museu do Chiado (➤ 51)

INFORMATION

- ✚ H8; alII
- ✉ São Carlos-Largo de São Carlos
- 🍴 Cafés, bars and restaurants
- Ⓖ Baixa-Chiado
- ▤ 58, 100; tram 15, 18, 28
- ♿ Poor
- ↔ Igreja de São Roque (➤ 38), Rossio (➤ 41), Bairro Alto (➤ 37)

Museu Arqueológico do Carmo

HIGHLIGHTS

- Church ruins
- Shrunken heads
- Mummies
- Gothic tombs
- Bronze Age pottery
- Tiles
- Prehistoric artefacts

INFORMATION

- ✚ H8; alII
- ✉ Convento do Carmo, Largo do Carmo
- ☎ 213 478 629
- 🕐 Apr–end Sep Tue–Sun 10–6; Oct–end Mar Tue–Sun 10–1. Closed public hols
- Ⓜ Baixa-Chiado
- 🚌 58, 100; tram 28. Elevador de Santa Justa
- ♿ Poor
- 💲 Moderate
- ↔ Chiado (► 39), Rossio (► 41), Baixa (► 42), Igreja de São Roque (► 38)

Metallurgy tools from Vila Nova de São Pedro hillfort, c3000 BC

Modern, well-organized museums such as the Gulbenkian are a joy, but there is something very appealing about the wonderfully jumbled and eccentric collection of exhibits in the Museu Arqueológico do Carmo.

Location The archaeological museum is within the ruins of the Convento do Carmo, a Carmelite convent built by Nun' Álvares Pereira. He was a general and companion-in-arms to João I at the Battle of Aljubarrota in 1385, which secured Portuguese independence from Castile for two hundred years. Until 1755 when the convent church was toppled by the Great Earthquake, it was the largest church in the city. Over the years its ruins were used as a grave-yard, municipal dump and military stable. Today its soaring Gothic interior is largely open to the Lisbon sky, the nave and chancel now a threadbare garden full of cats, flowers and shat-tered statuary.

Eccentric The museum's exhibits are a slightly disorganized and eccentric mixture, though none the worse for that, their eclectic jumble constituting part of their appeal. They include two large tombs, one belonging to Ferdinand I, King of Portugal from 1367 to 1382, the other to Gonçalo de Souza, chancellor to Henry the Navigator. The stone bust in the chancel is thought to be the oldest known image of Afonso Henriques, Portugal's first king. Older exhibits include prehistoric and Visigothic artefacts, notably flints, arrowheads and pottery, together with Roman remains and a large number of Hebrew, Arabic and other stone inscriptions. The more eccentric displays include shrunken heads, two South American mummies, and many tiles and florid pieces of sculpture.

Rossio

Every city has its main square, and Lisbon's is the Rossio. Though it is not the prettiest place to take a break—there is little greenery and a lot of traffic—it does appeal as a meeting place for visitors and locals alike.

Turbulent past The Rossio, also known as Praça Dom Pedro IV, is Lisbon's natural focus, a large and bustling square close to one of the city's main stations, the Chiado shopping district and the Baixa. It dates from around the 13th century, though its present appearance is due mostly to the Marquês de Pombal (▶17), and 19th-century rebuilding. Between 1534 and 1820 the Inquisitors' palace stood on the north side, and in the 16th century the Inquisitors' victims—convicted heretics—were burned in the square. The Inquisition's sentences were handed down from São Domingos, a church to the east, still closed after a fire in the 1950s.

Relaxing present Today the square is lined with cafés and shops, some of which have fine turn-of-the-century façades. Many of the cafés have outside tables, the best vantage points from which to watch the world go by. Two of the most popular cafés are Nicola (▶71) on the western flank of the square and Suiça (▶71) on the eastern side. The statue (1870) at the heart of the square is Dom Pedro IV, though it was sculpted as Maximilian of Mexico. It was passing through Lisbon on the way to Mexico, and remained when news broke of Maximilian's assassination. The square's grandest building, the Teatro Nacional de Dona Maria, was built in the 1840s on the site of the former Inquisitors' palace.

DID YOU KNOW?

- The Rossio is the most expensive property on the Portuguese Monopoly board

HIGHLIGHTS

- Cafés (▶69)
- Shop fronts
- Statue of Dom Pedro IV
- Fountain
- Teatro Nacional
- Façade of Estação do Rossio (station)

INFORMATION

- H8–J8; bIII
- Praça Dom Pedro IV
- Cafés, bars and restaurants
- Rossio
- All services to the Rossio
- Poor
- Baixa (▶42), Museu Arqueológico do Carmo (▶40), Chiado (▶39), Praça do Comércio (▶43)

Top: Rossio railway station's fine façade. Left: Statue of Dom Pedro IV

41

Baixa

HIGHLIGHTS

- Art deco shop fronts
- Mosaic pavements
- Cobbled streets

INFORMATION

- J8; bIII
- Streets between the Rossio and Praça do Comércio
- Cafés, bars and restaurants
- Rossio/Baixa-Chiado
- All services to the Rossio and Praça do Comércio
- Poor
- Praça do Comércio (➤ 43), Rossio (➤ 41), Sé (➤ 44), Castelo de São Jorge (➤ 45), Alfama (➤ 46)

The tiny Baixa district, lodged between the hills of the Chiado and Alfama, with its planned network of 18th-century cobbled streets, its many elaborate shop fronts and lively commercial bustle, forms the heart of old Lisbon.

Pombal's vision A grid of ordered streets, the Baixa district stretches from the Rossio in the north to the Praça do Comércio in the south, with the Chiado rising to the west and the Alfama to the east. It is thought this low-lying area was once centred on a stream, with houses built on stilts to escape flooding. Its appearance was changed beyond all recognition following the 1755 earthquake, when the Marquês de Pombal decided to rebuild the area along strictly rational lines (➤ 17). The forthright First Minister decreed that all new streets should be '40 feet in width, with pavements on either side protected from wheeled traffic by stone pillars, as in London'.

Tradition Pombal's dream was realized with the help of a military engineer, Eugénio dos Santos, and the result has been described by some as one of the finest European architectural achievements of the age. To others the district's relentless simplicity and symmetry made it appear bland and soulless. Today there is no denying the streets' lively old-fashioned charm, nor the appeal of the mosaic-patterned pavements, tiled façades and lovely old shop fronts. The pedestrianized Rua Augusta is the area's main axis. Many minor streets bear names relating to the trades once practised there—Rua da Prata (silversmiths), Rua Áurea (formerly Rua do Ouro —goldsmiths) and Rua dos Sapateiros (cobblers).

Restoration is reviving the Baixa's charm

Praça do Comércio

The Praça do Comércio, the focus of the Marquês de Pombal's reconstruction of 1758, is dominated by the statue of José I. It provides a triumphal entrance to the city from the airy open spaces of the waterfront.

Gateway Locally the square is known as the Terreiro do Paço, or Terrace of the Palace, an allusion to the 16th-century Royal Palace that stood here until it was almost completely destroyed by the 1755 earthquake. At its heart stands an equestrian statue of José I, king at the time of the 1755 earthquake, the blackened lustre of its bronze giving rise to the Praça's nickname 'Black Horse Square'. It took some 1,000 people almost four days to move the statue into position. The palace's old steps still climb up from the waterfront, but today the square is dominated by the vast, 19th-century triumphal arch on its northern flank, and by ranks of imposing arcades and neo-classical government offices. In 1908, King Carlos I was assassinated together with Luis Filipe, his son and heir, in the corner of the square near Rua do Arsenal.

Revival Now that the city authorities have banned its use as a carpark, the Praca do Comércio is once again one of Lisbon's most majestic squares. Its grand spaces and imposing buildings, once compromised, have been released from the motorcar's tyranny and the square can again reveal its intended effect—to serve as a dramatic gateway from the sea, and as an antechamber to the well-ordered streets of the Baixa and the rest of the city.

HIGHLIGHTS

- View from the waterfront
- Triumphal arch
- Arcades
- Statue of Dom José I

INFORMATION

- J8; bIV
- Praça do Comércio
- Terréiro do Paço/Baixa-Chiado
- All services to Praça do Comércio
- Good
- Free
- Baixa (► 42), Sé (► 44), Rossio (► 41), Castelo de São Jorge (► 45)

José I surveys the Praça do Comércio

43

Sé

HIGHLIGHTS

- Twin towers
- Rose window
- Baptismal font
- Bartolomeu Chapel (1324)
- Nativity, Joaquim Machado de Castro (1766)
- Tomb of Lopo Fernandes Pacheco
- Cloisters
- Treasury
- Reliquary of St. Vincent
- Dom José I monstrance

INFORMATION

- ✚ J8; cIII
- ✉ Largo da Sé
- ☎ 218 866 752
- 🕐 Cathedral: Tue–Sat 9–7, Mon, Sun and public hols 9–5. Cloister: May–Sep Tue–Sat 10–6.30, Mon 10–5; Oct–Apr Mon–Sat 10–5. Closed Sun and public/religious hols
- ▣ Terréiso do Paço
- 🚌 37; tram 12, 28
- ♿ Poor
- 🎫 Cathedral: free Cloister: inexpensive
- 🔄 Praça do Comércio (➤ 43), Baixa (➤ 42), Castelo de São Jorge (➤ 45)

Above: *The Romanesque front of the Sé*

Nothing evokes a stronger sense of Lisbon's long history than views of the formidable cathedral, whose ancient stone towers can be seen above the rooftops from the Baixa and the viewpoints of the Bairro Alto.

History Lisbon's cathedral was begun around 1150, soon after Afonso Henriques, Portugal's first king, had captured the city from the Moors. It was the city's first church, and legend claims it stands on the site of a mosque. Like other Portuguese cathedrals of similar vintage—Évora, Porto, Coimbra—it has a fortress-like appearance, the result of its plain Romanesque design

and the tumultuous times in which it was built, when there was still a threat from the Moors. Much of its original shell survives, notably its distinctive squat towers, which unlike the old chancel, withstood the earthquakes of 1344 and 1755, as well as the attentions of restorers.

Interior On the left as you enter the church is a font, reputedly used in 1195 to baptise St. Antony of Padua, who was born in Lisbon. The first chapel on the left is decorated with an intricately carved Nativity scene, the work of 18th-century sculptor Joaquim Machado de Castro. More beautiful still is the tomb of Lopo Fernandes Pacheco, a courtier of Afonso IV, in the chapel on the right of the gothic ambulatory. The ruined 13th-century Gothic cloister is worth seeing for its lovely sculptural fragments.

Castelo de São Jorge

Every city needs at least one place like Lisbon's ancient fortress. With its breathtaking views and lovely gardens, its a shady oasis where you can retreat from the rigours of sightseeing to enjoy some peace and quiet.

Defence Lisbon's evocative castle marks the city's birthplace, the spot where Phoenician traders probably first made camp, attracted by the area's fine natural harbour, its easily defended position and the agricultural potential of its fertile hinterland. Later it was fortified by the Romans, Visigoths and Moors, the defeat of the last, at the hands of Afonso Henriques in 1147, marking a turning point in the campaign to oust the Moors from Portugal. Henriques took the fortress after a 17-week siege, a victory tainted by the behaviour of his British and French allies—supposedly Christian Crusaders—who ran amok, pillaging and murdering Moors and Christians alike.

Views Today the castle's walls have been rather over-restored. Its pristine stonework makes it hard to believe that much of the 12th-century original remains, though its lofty site and beautiful grounds are irresistible. The outer walls enclose the little district of Santa Cruz, one of the medieval jewels of the old Alfama district. A statue of Afonso Henriques glowers over the main entrance, beyond which lies a lovely array of verdant terraces and leafy walkways. Ducks and swans glide across limpid pools, while other birds, some exotic, flit across the manicured lawns. The castle also contains Olisipónia, an interpretive and multimedia centre. Best of all, however, are the superlative views over the rooftops from the old Moorish battlements, which rise over 30m above the Alfama.

DID YOU KNOW?

- Portugal's early kings occupied the Alcáçova, the castle's former Moorish palace
- The castle's name, São Jorge (St. George), reputedly commemorates the Anglo-Portuguese pact of 1371
- The Portuguese call the castle belvedere the 'ancient window', because of its views

HIGHLIGHTS

- Views
- Gardens
- Battlements and towers
- Olisipónia multimedia show
- Parade ground

INFORMATION

- ➕ J8; cIII
- ✉ Rua Costa do Castelo
- 🕐 Apr–Sep daily 9–8/9; Oct–Mar daily 9–6/7
- 🚋 37; tram 12, 28
- ♿ Poor
- 🎫 Castle: free. Olisipónia: moderate
- 🔄 Alfama (➤ 46), Museu das Artes Decorativas (➤ 47), Baixa (➤ 42), Rossio (➤ 41), Sé (➤ 44), Campo de Santa Clara (➤ 48)

Alfama

HIGHLIGHTS

- Castelo de São Jorge
- Church of São Miguel
- Church of Santo Estevão
- Church of Santa Luzia
- Pátio das Flores
- Largo de São Rafael
- Largo das Portas do Sol
- Miradouro de Santa Luzia
- Rua São Miguel

This warren of atmospheric old streets is tailor-made for random exploration. The narrow alleys, hanging washing, flower-laden windows and beautifully preserved tile-fronted mansions are like an image from the past.

Springs Of all Lisbon's old quarters, none is more evocative or pleasant to explore than the Alfama, a labyrinth of timeless vignettes and Medina-like streets that still have an Arabic feel. The area takes its name from a Moorish word, *alhama*, or fountain, a reference to the hot springs in Largo das Alcaçarías. As a distinct enclave, however, it is much older, probably dating back to the first Phoenician or Roman traders who settled in the are around the present-day Castelo. Between 711 and 1147 it became an important Moorish suburb, and later the home of the city's first churches. In time it became a retreat for the city's élite, losing its cachet only after the 1755 earthquake.

Top: *Walks depicted in tiles*

INFORMATION

- ✚ J8–K8; cII–cIII
- ✉ Around Castelo de São Jorge
- 🍴 Cafés, bars and restaurants
- 🚇 Rossio/Martim Moniz
- 🚌 37; tram 12, 28
- ♿ Poor
- ↔ Museu das Artes Decorativas (➤ 47)
- ❓ Avoid the area after dark

Sights Today for the most part the area is a robust and old-fashioned residential neighbourhood, though the restorers, gentrifying many of the once humble dwellings, the restaurants and the first trendy shops are beginning to take the edge off its pristine appeal. The best way to see the district is to wander at random amid the streets and half-hidden squares—maps are almost useless here. Streets you might try to head for include the Rua de São Pedro, Rua São Miguel, Beco de Cardosa, the Pátio das Flores, Largo de São Rafael and Rua dos Remédios. Try also to take in the viewpoints at Largo das Portas do Sol and the Miradouro de Santa Luzia, which has several good cafés.

Museu das Artes Decorativas

This beautifully restored 17th-century palace has a stunning collection of furniture, carpets and antiques displayed in a period setting, giving the visitor a picture of upper-class Lisbon life in the 18th and 19th centuries.

Bequest Lisbon's beguiling Museum of the Decorative Arts is housed in the 17th-century palace of the Counts of Azurara, former home of Ricardo do Espírito Santo Silva (1900–1955) a Portuguese philanthropist. He left the house and his private collection of art and artefacts to the nation in 1953. Both house and collection, run by the Espírito Santo Silva Foundation, are now open to the public. The foundation also supports a series of workshops (next door to the museum) in which you can watch people practising traditional skills such as bookbinding, gilding, wood-carving and cabinet-making.

Exquisite home Santo Silva had exceptional taste, with the result that his collection embraces some of the finest examples of Portuguese and other art and artefacts. The palace itself is beautiful with its original 17th-century wooden floors, painted ceilings and panels of blue and white *azulejos* (tiles). This forms the perfect setting for the lovely furniture, antiques, tapestries and rugs from Arraiolos, the latter from a central Portueuse town renowned for its exquisite carpets. Also on display are porcelain and silverware, together with various *objets d'art* of both Portuguese and Indo-Portuguese origin. Perhaps the most captivating areas of the museum to visit are the bedrooms, complete with tiny four-poster beds, and the upstairs dining room, with its grandfather clock and fine painted ceiling.

HIGHLIGHTS

- Palace
- Furniture
- Carpets
- Painted ceilings
- Bedrooms
- Tapestries
- Silverware
- Inlaid chess table

INFORMATION

- ✚ J8; cIII
- ✉ Largo das Portas do Sol 2
- ☎ 218 814 600
- 🕐 Tue–Sun 10–5. Closed public hols
- 🍴 Café
- 🚇 Rossio
- 🚌 37; tram 12, 28
- ♿ Very poor: many stairs
- 💰 Expensive
- ↔ Alfama (➤ 46), Campo de Santa Clara (➤ 48), Castelo de São Jorge (➤ 45)

Above: *The palace is a superb setting.* Top: *Portuguese silverware*

Campo de Santa Clara

HIGHLIGHTS

- Feira da Ladra
- Santa Engrácia
- São Vicente de Fora
- Jardim Boto Machado
- Miradouro da Senhora do Monte
- Museu Nacional Militar

INFORMATION

- K7
- Campo de Santa Clara
- Feira da Ladra: Tue 7am–1pm; Sat 7am–4pm
- Cafés
- 12, 37, 104, 105, 107 and then walk; tram 28 direct
- Poor
- Museu das Artes Decorativas (► 47), Alfama (► 46)
- Watch for pickpockets

Campo de Santa Clara deserves a special mention for its churches, but should preferably be visited on a market day when stalls are set up by individuals selling anything from shoe insoles to used car batteries.

Lively market Campo de Santa Clara lies on the eastern margins of the Alfama district, one of Lisbon's most atmospheric quarters. The square and its surrounding streets are best known for their flea market, the Feira da Ladra (the 'Thieves' Market'), which takes place here on Tuesday morning and all day Saturday. The Feira's covered stalls (in the middle of the square) sell a predictable assortment of market goods—food, shoes, cheap clothes and household items—while the peripheral stalls deal in books, old postcards and miscellaneous bric-a-brac. Don't be fooled; genuine bargains are hard to find, but you can spend an enjoyable morning browsing here.

Vistas Market or no, the area around Campo de Santa Clara would still be worth exploring. Two of the city's more interesting churches are near by: Santa Engrácia (► 56) to the southeast and São Vicente de Fora (► 57) to the northwest, the former completed only in 1966, the latter of 1704, the burial place of many of Portugal's kings and queens. At the heart of the square itself is the Jardim Boto Machado, a small garden full of palms and exotic plants, with a fine view over the city to the south. To the north are the Palácio Lavradio, home to the military tribunal, and another excellent viewpoint, the Miradouro da Senhora do Monte. A short walk to the south of the square is the Museu Nacional Militar, the military museum, in the 18th-century former arsenal (► 54).

The popular flea market held in the Campo de Santa Clara

Igreja da Madre de Deus

This church has some of the city's most opulent decoration. Its lavish gilt baroque pulpit and altar, and walls covered with tiles and 16th–17th century paintings, make it an enticing double bill when seen with the adjoining Museu Nacional do Azulejo.

Convent Like Belém to the west, this grand and sumptuously decorated church, some 3km east of the Baixa, is one of the few sights in Lisbon worth leaving the heart of the city to see. Originally part of a larger convent, it was founded in 1509 by Dona Leonor, widow of Dom João II. Later it was expanded by João III, only to be virtually destroyed during the 1755 earthquake. Subsequent rebuilding turned the church's interior into one of the most magnificent in the city, but the exterior's Manueline doorway and the crypt (with a grandiose altar and 16th-century Seville tiles) have survived from Leonor's earlier foundation.

Elaborate church The interior is a masterpiece of decorative excess, laden with gilt wood and tiles and decorated with several glorious paintings. Scenes from the Life of the Virgin fill the coffered main vault, paintings high on the walls depict scenes from the Life of St. Francis (right wall when facing the altar) and the Life of St. Clare (left wall when facing altar). The lower walls are covered in beautiful blue and white 18th-century Dutch tiles. In the even more breathtaking chapter house, virtually every surface is adorned with tiles or gilt-framed paintings. Also make a point of seeing the Capela de Santo António and the sacristy, which are similarly embellished.

HIGHLIGHTS

- Manueline doorway
- Gilt woodwork
- Vault paintings
- Wall paintings
- Chapter house
- Sacristy
- Capela de Santo António
- Crypt

INFORMATION

- L6
- Rua da Madre de Deus 4
- 218 147 747
- Wed–Sun 10–6, Tue 2–6
- 18, 42, 59, 104, 105
- Poor
- Free
- Museu Nacional do Azulejo (➤ 50)

The main altar in its gilded glory

Museu Nacional do Azulejo

- Tiled Manueline cloisters
- Café
- Lisbon cityscape (1738)
- Tiled Nativity (1580)
- Food tiles
- Modern Metro tiles
- Tiled battle scenes

INFORMATION

www.mnazulejo-ipmuseus.pt
- L6
- Rua da Madre de Deus 4
- 218 100 340/218 147 747
- Wed–Sun 10–6, Tue 2–6
- Café
- 18, 42, 59, 104, 105
- Poor
- Inexpensive. Free on Sun and public hols until 2
- Igreja da Madre de Deus (➤ 49)

This lovely museum in a tranquil monastic cloisters, traces the history of tile-making. Through Dutch, Moorish and Hispanic influences, here you'll see the Portuguese emerge as masters of their craft.

Simple and sophisticated The museum's earliest *azulejos* (a corruption of the Arabic word *azraq* (azure) or *zalayja*, meaning a smooth stone or polished terracotta) date from the beginning of the 16th century. Later exhibits show how simple, single-colour designs gave way to more sophisticated patterning allowed by the new majolica techniques imported from Italy. As the art developed, *azulejos* became still more complex and colourful. Later still, they were influenced by the single-motif patterns of Dutch tiles and by the fashion for blue and white inspired by the arrival of Ming dynasty porcelain in Europe. Simpler designs also resulted from the 1755 earthquake, when large numbers of cheap decorative tiles were required for rebuilding.

Museum highlights The museum is full of beautiful examples but look out in particular for the 38m-tiled cityscape of Lisbon, made in 1738 prior to the 1755 earthquake, and the small Manueline cloister decorated with its original 16th- and 17th-century tiles. Also, don't miss the fine, 16th-century polychrome tile picture of Nossa Senhora da Vida, a nativity scene. There are delightful 18th-century blue-and-white tile scenes of every day life such as a doctor giving an injection. Further displays depict battle scenes, and there is a collection of modern Metro tiles by well-known artists such as Julio Pomar and Viera da Silva. The museum restaurant is decorated with mouth-watering food *azulejos* depicting hams, rabbits and other delicacies.

The 18th-century tiled cityscape of Lisbon

LISBON's
best

MUSEU DE ARTE POPULAR

Museums

TWENTIETH-CENTURY DESIGN

As well as being the home to temporary exhibitions and performing arts, the immense and outstanding Centro Cultural de Belém has added another museum to its collection, the Museo do Design. The museum is divided into three sections entitled Luxury, Pop and Cool, and illustrates the forms, concepts and function of objects from the 20th century. ✚ B10 ✉ Praça do Império ☎ 213 612 934; www.ccbpt 🕙 Daily 11–8 🚌 27, 28, 29, 43, 49, 51; tram 15 🚊 Belém (Cascais line) from Cais do Sodré 💶 Moderate

MUSEU NACIONAL DE ARTE POPULAR

Lisbon's National Folk Art Museum is near the waterfront in Belém. It was established in 1948 and its typical postwar utilitarian architecture makes it a bit dated, but there are enough interesting exhibits to merit a quick visit. It looks at Portugal's folk art and traditions province by province, with five rooms of clothes, paintings, rugs, votive offerings, musical instruments, agricultural implements, pottery, wickerwork and other craft items. The exhibits are complemented by photographs and striking wall paintings, the latter the work of leading modern Portuguese artists such as Paulo Ferreira, Carlos Botelho and Tomás de Melo.
✚ B10 ✉ Avenida de Brasília ☎ 213 011 282 🕙 Tue–Sun 10–12.30, 2–5 🚌 27, 28, 43, 49, 51; tram 15 💶 Inexpensive. Free Sun morning ❓ Access from Mosteiro dos Jerónimos is via the waterfront and a subway under the road and railway

Exhibits in the Museu de Arte Popular are backed by photographs and paintings

MUSEU DA CIÊNCIA

Permanent hands-on science exhibits along with temporary thematic exhibitions all help to make science more accessible. Check out the antique scientific instrument display.
⊞ G/H7 ⊠ Rua da Escola Politécnica 56-58 ☎ 213 921 808; www.museu-dacienca.ul.pt 🕙 Mon–Fri 10–1, Sat 3–6 🚇 Rato 🚌 15, 58; tram 24 💶 Inexpensive. Free on Sat

MUSEU DO CHIADO

In a 13th-century abbey, this museum is devoted to Portguese painting and sculpture. It was refurbished in 1994 with dramatic high brick vaults and polished grey marble, by the French architect Jean-Michel Wilmotte. Concentrating on the years 1850–1950 it delves into realism, romanticism, symbolism and modernism. Worth seeing are *A Sesta* by Almada Negreiros; the *Concerto de Amadores* by Columbano; and Soares dos Reis's *O Desterrado*.
⊞ H8 ⊠ Rua Serpa Pinto 6 ☎ 213 432 148/9; www.museudochiado-ipmuseus.pt 🕙 Wed–Sun 10–6, Tue 2–6
🍴 Café 🚌 58, 100; tram 28 💶 Moderate. Free Sun and public hols until 2

A Sesta, *Almada Negreiros (1939)*

MUSEU DA CIDADE

The Museum of the City lies north of the heart of the city in the northwest corner of the Campo Grande. A stimulating museum in a lovely setting, it uses paintings, prints and drawings to trace the development of Lisbon through the centuries. Highlights include a model of pre-earthquake Lisbon, a 17th-century painting showing the Praça do Comércio before the Marqués de Pombal remodelled it, and a picture of the poet Fernando Pessoa, painted in 1954, 19 years after his death.
⊞ G3 ⊠ Campo Grande 245 ☎ 217 513 200 🕙 Tue–Sun 10–1, 2–6 🚇 Campo Grande 🚌 1, 3, 7, 33, 36, 47, 50 💶 Moderate. Free on Sun

MUSEU ETNOLÓGICO DA SOCIEDADE DE GEOGRAFIA

This little gem in the middle of the city displays objects from Portugal's former colonies in Africa and Asia, in a remarkable late 19th-century room. Opening times are limited.
⊞ H7; all ⊠ Rua das Portas de Santo Antão 100 ☎ 213 425 068; www.http://socgeografia-lisboa.plantetaclik.pt 🕙 Mon, Wed, Fri 11–1, 3–6 🚇 Restauradores 🚌 1, 2, 9, 21, 44, 45 💶 Inexpensive

MUSEU DAS MARIONETAS

This fascinating museum displays indigenous puppets from Japan, Thailand, Burma and Indonesia. There are also occasional puppet shows. The museum has moved from its previous dowdy home to this beautifully restored 17th-century building, the Converto das Bernardas.
⊞ J8; clll ⊠ Rua da Esperanca 146 ☎ 213 942 810 🕙 Wed–Sun 10–1, 2–6 🚌 37; tram 28 💶 Inexpensive

MUSEUM IN A PALACE

The Palácio Pimenta provides the graceful setting for the Museu da Cidade. Built in the 18th century, during the reign of the free-spending Dom João V, the palace is distinguished by its *azulejos*. In the kitchen, these depict fish, swans, hares and other creatures hung upside down on the walls. In the upstairs rooms, a ring of dado tiles reveals each room's original function.

53

MUSEU DA MÚSICA

A collection of musical instruments from around Europe dating from the 16th to 20th centuries. 🚩 E3 ✉ Rua João Freitas Branco ☎ 217 710 990; www.museudamusic-ipmuseus.pt 🕐 Tue–Sat 10–6 🚇 Alto dos Moihos 💷 Inexpensive. Under 14s free.

Vasco da Gama in the Discovery Room of the Museu Nacional Militar

MUSEU NACIONAL MILITAR

The National Military Museum is on the site of a 16th-century shipyard. Following a fire and the 1755 earthquake, the complex was rebuilt as an arsenal, becoming the Artillery Museum in 1851. Today, as well as an artillery collection—one of the world's best—the museum also has extensive displays of guns, pistols and swords. Among them are Portuguese pieces dating back to the 16th century, together with artefacts of French, Dutch, English, Spanish and Arab origin. Other highlights include the armoury, paintings on military themes and large spreads of tiles portraying battle scenes. 🚩 K8 ✉ Caminhos de Ferro-Largo do Museu da Artilharia ☎ 218 882 300; www.geira.pt/mmilitar 🕐 Tue–Sun 10–5 🚌 9, 25, 28, 35, 39, 46 💷 Moderate. Free Wed

MUSEU NACIONAL DO TEATRO

The National Theatre Museum concentrates on the personalities who have graced the Lisbon stage over the years, which makes it of limited interest to the casual visitor. It is worth a look if you are visiting the neighbouring Costume Museum, though, as it also has theatrical costumes, props, photographs, stage designs and other theatrical ephemera. 🚩 F1 ✉ Parque de Monteiro-Mor, Estrada do Lumiar 10 ☎ 217 567 410; www.museudoteatro-ipmuseus.pt 🕐 Wed–Sun 10–6, Tue 2–6 (closes at 5 in winter). Closed public hols 🚌 1,3, 4, 7, 36, 101, 108 💷 Moderate; joint ticket with Museo Nacional do Traje. Free Sun after 2pm

MUSEU NACIONAL DO TRAJE

The National Museum of Costume occupies the tiled and frescoed Palácio do Duque de Palmela, also known as the Palácio Monteiro-Mor, in the Parque do Monteiro-Mor at Lumiar. Visit the Jardim Botânico, dotted with pools, plants and trees in a rugged hilly setting, as well as the museum itself, which has beautiful old tapestries, jewels, toys and costumes. 🚩 F1 ✉ Parque de Monteiro-Mor, Largo Júlio de Castilho ☎ 217 590 318; www.museudotraje-impmuseus.pt 🕐 Tue–Sun 10–6 (closes at 5 in winter) 🚌 1, 3, 4, 7 36, 101, 106, 107, 108 💷 Moderate; joint ticket with Museo Nacional do Teatro

PUPPET POLITICS

Puppets in Portugal have been used for many years as powerful tools of political satire and subversion. They became especially popular during the 18th century, when puppet operas were used to poke fun at and explore the social and political affairs of the day. During the Salazar dictatorship they were banned altogether.

Views

CASTELO DE SÃO JORGE
The castle's terraces, and the castle parade in particular, provide extensive city-wide panoramas.
J8; cIII ⊠ Rua Costa do Castelo 🚍 Rossio 🚍 37; tram 28

MIRADOURO DE SÃO PEDRO DE ALCÂNTARA
Perched on the edge of the Bairro Alto, this belvedere offers sweeping views of the Rossio and Baixa below. Part of the fun of coming here is to travel the old Elevador da Glória, built in 1885.
H7; all ⊠ Rua São Pedro de Alcântara 🚍 Restauradores
🚍 58, 100; tram 24 or Glória elevator

MIRADOURO DE SANTA LUZIA
This little area was laid out purely as a viewpoint (*miradouro* in Portuguese). The panorama extends across old rooftops to the harbour and river beyond.
J8; cIII ⊠ Largo de Santa Luzia 🚍 Rossio 🚍 37; tram 28

PONTE 25 DE ABRIL
If you are driving from the south you will cross Lisbon's 2-km suspension bridge; a panorama view embraces the Tagus and a large part of the old city.
E10 ⊠ Avenida da Ponte 🚍 Alcântara 🚍 52, 53

TORRE VASCO DA GAMA
The 140-m Vasco da Gama tower at the Parco das Nações is Lisbon's highest point; the views are superb. Cable cars run between the tower and Olivias Marina Locks and there is a restaurant at the top.
M2 ⊠ Parco das Nações ☎ 218 918 000 🕐 Jun–end Sep Mon–Fri 11–8, Sat–Sun, public hols 10–9; Oct–end May Mon–Fri 11–7, Sat–Sun, public hols 10–8 🚍 Oriente 💷 One-way moderate; round-trip expensive

MORE VIEWPOINTS

The Santa Justa elevator (H8; bIII) gives a close-up view of the Baixa. Largo de Santo Estêvão in the Alfama (J8) has views of the river, across rooftops crowded with TV aerials. Try the Miradouro da Nossa Senhora do Monte (K7), north of Campo de Santa Clara (➤ 48); the Miradouro da Santa Catarina (H8), in the Bairro Alto; and Parque Eduardo VII (G6, ➤ 60), whose northern flanks overlook the old city. The Torre de Belém (B10, ➤ 26) and ferries (➤ 19 and 59) give views of and from the river.

Lisbon seen from the Castelo de São Jorge

Churches

Igreja de Santa Engrácia

SANTO ANTÓNIO DE LISBOA

This little church stands on the site of the house where St. Antony was born in 1195. Built after the 1755 earthquake, it contains paintings by Pedro de Carvalho, who was responsible for the decoration of many churches after the disaster. The square in which the church and the cathedral sit is called Santo António de Sé because the church is immediately in front of the cathedral. A small museum displays objects related to the saint's life.

➕ J8; bIII ✉ Largo de Santo António de Sé 24 ☎ 218 860 447 🕐 Church daily 8–7.30. Museum Tue–Sun 10–1, 2–6. Closed public hols 🚌 37; tram 28 💷 Church free. Museum inespensive

SANTA ENGRÁCIA

The church of Santa Engrácia is in the Alfama close to São Vicente de Fora. It is the Panteão Nacional, or National Pantheon. The large baroque building, begun in 1682, survived the 1755 earthquake, but was not completed until 1966 when the cupola was finally added. The fact that this project took 284 years to complete has led to a little Portuguese idiom —*obras de Santa Engrácia*—used as a synonym for delayed or unfinished work. The early design (by João Antunes) focuses on a balanced Greek Cross with four towers and curving arms, and was influenced by new departures in Italian baroque architecture of the period. The result is a slightly chill and over-precise building, its appearance well suited to its memorial function. Among the people buried here are several Portuguese presidents, the poets Guerra Junqueiro and João de Deus, and writer Almeida Garrett, one of Portugal's leading 19th-century literary figures; the Chiado's Rua Garrett is named in his honour.

➕ K8 ✉ Campo de Santa Clara ☎ 218 876 629 🕐 Tue–Sun 10–5 🚌 12, 34, 104, 105, 107; tram 28 💷 Inexpensive. Free Sun

SANTA LUZIA

The reason to visit this modest church is obvious from the outside. Its exterior walls are covered in *azulejos* depicting Lisbon before and after the earthquake of 1755, and its garden is laid out as a charming viewpoint, the Miradouro de Santa Luzia (► 55).

➕ J8; cIII ✉ Largo de Santa Luzia 🚇 Rossio 🚌 37; tram 28

ST. ANTONY

Although St. Vincent is patron saint of Lisbon, St. Antony of Padua is the city's unofficial patron saint, as well as the much-venerated patron saint of Portugal. He is buried in Padua in Italy, but was born Fernando de Bulhoês in Lisbon, where the church of Santo Antonio de Lisboa now stands. The saint is revered as a matchmaker, protector of young brides and patron of the lost and found. His feast day, widely celebrated in Lisbon, is 12 June (► 24).

NOSSA SENHORA DA CONCEIÇAO VELHA

Like Santa Luzia, this is one to enjoy from the outside. Most of the church collapsed in 1755, but the south doorway survived as a fine and rare exmple of the Manueline style—the ornate form of gothic associated with the reign of Manuel I (1495–1521) when wealth poured into Portugal.

🔲 J8 ✉ Rua da Alfândega 🚌 104, 105; tram 15, 25, 28

SÃO VICENTE DE FORA

'St. Vincent Outside the Walls' was indeed outside the city walls when it was built between 1582 and 1627, over the site of a 12th-century church erected to commemorate the Crusaders' victory over the Moors. The construction of the present church took place during Portugal's period of subjugation to the Spanish, and was the work of Philip II of Spain's principal architect, the Italian Filippo Terzi. His cupola was felled by the 1755 earthquake and has been replaced by a more modest dome, though the majestic nave survives, its highlights a glorious coffered vault and extravagant baroque altar. The monastery and cloisters (through a gate to the right of the façade) are adorned with lovely 18th-century *azulejos* depicting rustic, court and hunting scenes from La Fontaine's Fables. Off the cloisters the former refectory serves as Portugal's Royal Pantheon, which since 1855 has been the resting place of the tombs of most of the country's Bragança kings and queens from Dom João IV (died 1656) to Dom Carlos (assassinated 1908). The large *azulujo* panel depicts the taking of Lisbon from the Moors in 1147.

🔲 J8, cll ✉ Rua Voz do Operário-Rua São Vicente ☎ 218 824 400 🕐 Tue–Sun 9–12.30, 3–6 🚌 12; tram 28 ♿ Church free. Monastery inexpensive

ST. VINCENT

When São Vicente, or St. Vincent, was martyred in Valencia, his body was taken by boat, reputedly under the guidance of two ravens, to the desolate headland in southwest Portugal now known as Cabo de São Vicente (Cape St. Vincent). The ravens were seen again in 1173, when the saint's relics were removed to Lisbon on the orders of Afonso Henriques, Portugal's founding king. Vincent became the city's patron saint, and the ravens appear in the city's crest.

The tiled sacristy of São Vicente de Fora

57

Parks & Gardens

WALK UP THE AVENUE

Avenida da Liberdade cuts a 1500-m, tree-lined swathe from the Rossio north to the Praça Marquês de Pombal junction, where Parque Eduardo VII begins. This is Lisbon's grandest road, and inevitably invites comparison with the Champs Elysées in Paris. Though no peaceful green oasis, it is well worth a stroll for its trees, water features, pavement mosaics, 19th-century buildings and outdoor cafés.

A fountain in the Jardim Guerra Junqueiro—the Jardim da Estrela

CASTELO DE SÃO JORGE

The highlights of Lisbon's ancient citadel are the views from its ramparts and the lovely expanses of lawns and gardens laid out in and around its walls. Birds wander around many of them, exotic and most of them quite tame, while ducks and other waterfowl dive and dabble in the garden's many ponds and fountains. There are also plenty of benches and picnic tables.

➕ J8; cIII ✉ Rua Costa do Castelo 🕐 Apr–end Sep daily 9–8/9; Oct–end Mar daily 9–6/7 🚌 37; tram 12, 28 🎟 Free

JARDIM BOTÂNICO

Lisbon's principal botanical gardens spread across a hilly slope just above the busy Avenida da Liberdade. An oasis of calm in frantic surroundings, they are—with the Parque Eduardo VII and Castelo de São Jorge gardens—the areas of green space you should make a special point of seeing if your time in the city is limited. Laid out in 1873, they are still the responsibility of the Faculdade das Ciências (Faculty of Sciences), whose slightly decrepit building you pass on the main way in, along a palm-lined alley. Mazes of little paved paths wind downhill, wending their way past masses of exotic plants and trees (some 10,000 plants in total), all clearly labelled. A couple of small, fish-filled lakes enhance the scene. The back entrance on Rua da Algeria is closed on weekends.

➕ H7 ✉ Rua Escola Politécnica-Rua da Alegria ☎ 213 921 800 🕐 Daily 9–7 🚇 Avenida/Rato 🚌 58, 100 🎟 Inexpensive

JARDIM GUERRA JUNQUEIRO

This easy-going park is better known locally as the Jardim da Estrela after the Basílica da Estrela (▶ 34), which lies immediately to the south. A neighbourhood park, it is a much visited by mothers and children, with plenty of specially designated areas for kids to play in. Adults can sit and watch the goings-on from the comfort of shaded benches. There are elm and plane trees, with little enclosed flower-beds providing patches of colour, and a small duck-dotted lake (with a nice adjacent café), which serves as the park's natural focus. There is also an attractive wrought-iron gazebo, and on summer afternoons you may be lucky enough to catch one of the occasional brass band concerts.

➕ G7–G8 ✉ Calçada da Estrela 🕐 7–midnight 🍴 Café 🚇 Rato 🚌 9, 20, 22, 27, 38; tram 25, 28 🎟 Free

JARDIM ZOOLÓGICO DE LISBOA

Lisbon's zoo (➤ 62) may be somewhat lacklustre, but it is an appealing area in the former Parque das Laranjeiras, an old estate whose rose gardens, ponds and formal flower-beds have been carefully preserved among the animals. The upper, northern part of the park is wilder and less cultivated, with places for picnics and leisurely exploration, although you do have to pay to go into the zoo itself. In particular the Miradouro dos Moinhos (the Mill Belvedere) provides a broad panorama across much of the Monsanto park and the rest of the city. The park also has an eccentric little cemetery for dogs.

F4 ✉ Estrada de Benfica 158–60–Parque dos Laranjeiras ☎ 217 232 900; www.zoo.sapo.it ⏲ Apr–end Sep daily 10–8; Oct–end Mar daily 10–6 🍴 Café 🚇 Jardim Zoológico–Sete Rios 🚌 16, 26, 31, 41, 46, 54, 55, 58 💰 Expensive

PALÁCIO DOS MARQUÊSES DE FRONTEIRA

This wonderful palace lies in the northeast corner of the Parque Florestal de Monsanto (see ➤ 60), secreted away amid lovely gardens that provide a buffer against the rather ugly modern neighbourhood nearby. Although laid out to an Italian Renaissance plan, the gardens' vast numbers of *azulejos* (decorative tiles) give them an unmistakably Portuguese flavour. Virtually every possible patch of wall, terrace and fountain has been adorned with tiles, their blues and greens complementing natural colour of the water, trees and plants.

E5 ✉ Largo de São Domingos de Benfica 1 ☎ 217 782 023 ⏲ Guided tours: Jun–end Sep 4 daily; Oct–end May 2 daily (but check for latest details) 🚇 Sete Rios 🚌 72 💰 Moderate

Topiary in the garden of the Fronteira Palace

CATS

The Palácio dos Marquêses de Fronteira has some striking cats among its exterior tile decorations. This is apt for Lisbon, which has a large population of cats, many of them feral but fed by local people, who tend to be well disposed towards their feline neighbours.

59

COOL AND HOT

The Estufa Fria (Cool House) at Parque Eduardo VII has humid and perfumed halls filled with exotic flowers, shrubs and trees from across the globe. Numerous pathways weave past indoor ponds, fountains, streams and waterfalls, all full of fish, statues and pretty stones. The Estufa Quente (Hot House) opens off the Estufa Fria and has many of the same elements, but here the plants and temperatures are tropical and the air is filled with the twitter of bird song. Off the Hot House is a Cactus House crammed with many hundreds of exotic cacti of all shapes and sizes.

PARQUE EDUARDO VII

Lisbon's foremost park is Parque Eduardo VII at the northern end of the grand Avenida da Liberdade. Officially opened in 1902, it was named in honour of King Edward VII of Britain, who visited Portugal that year to reconfirm the age-old Anglo-Portuguese alliance (first signed in 1386). The park revolves around two broad, mosaic-paved boulevards, which in turn are intersected by tiny walkways and carefully manicured little hedgerows. Off to the east is the large neo-baroque Pavilhão dos Desportos, a sports pavilion recently repainted and renamed in honour of the Olympic marathon champion Carlos Lopes. Its tile panels depict battle scenes from Portugal's wars of independence against the Moors and Spanish. There are panoramic views from Rua Alamada Cardeal Cerejeira on the northern side, and wonderful cool and hot houses, lovely places to spend a tranquil half an hour away from the city's bustle and fumes (see panel this page).

✚ G6 ✉ Praça Marquês de Pombal ☎ Cool and hot houses 213 882 278 🕐 Cool and hot houses: Apr–end Sep daily 9–5.30; Oct–end Mar daily 9–4.30 🍴 Café Ⓜ Parque, Marquês de Pombal or São Sebastião 🚌 1, 2, 12, 20, 22, and many other services to Praça Marquês de Pombal 🅿 Park free. Cool and hot houses inexpensive

PARQUE FLORESTAL DE MONSANTO

This enormous area of parkland on the western fringes of Lisbon is probably the city's most positive legacy of Salazar but it is not recommended for walking. It is poorly kept and overgrown—its size makes maintenance a problem—and some parts are distinctly dangerous and insalubrious by day or night. Furthermore, the prominent Forte de Monsanto is used as a prison. However, if you have transport it is worth visiting for the public tennis courts, the running track and the children's playground, and there are fine views from the Miradouro de Monsanto and Miradouro dos Montes Claros.

✚ A5–E5–9 ✉ West of Avenida de Ceuta 🕐 Always open 🅿 Free

Strelitzia in the Parque Eduardo VII

Free Sights

OLD DISTRICTS

Lisbon is such a cheap city relative to most western European capitals that it is hard to begrudge the almost universally low admission charges to many of its key sights. It is also overflowing with pleasures that require no outlay save a little time. Chief among these is wandering in the city's older quarters—the Bairro Alto (► 37), Chiado (► 39), Baixa (► 42) and Alfama (► 46).

CHURCHES

There is no charge for visiting Lisbon's many ornate churches, although you may be required to pay a small fee to see areas such as the treasury. The most notable churches are the Igreja de São Roque (► 38), the Sé (cathedral, ► 44), and Igreja da Madre de Deus (► 49).

VIEWS

Lisbon has several named *miradouros* and other viewpoints (► 55), and you will find others by just wandering. City views can be had for next to nothing by crossing the Tagus on one of the ferries from the Cais de Alfândega on the main Praça do Comércio, especially if you then take a ride to the top of the Cristo Rey statue. There are three basic crossings: to Calcilhas, Barreiro and Montijo. Tickets are extremely cheap, and views of the river and city are superb on all three routes. You could also make a ferry-boat trip from Belém, from where services run to Trafaria.

Old streets run down from the heights

SQUARES AND PARKS

For the price of a drink you can sit at an outside café in one of Lisbon's great squares and watch the world go by. The Rossio (► 41) and Praça dos Restauradores spring most readily to mind. Or find a more intimate perch in one of the old-world cafés in the Chiado or Bairro Alto (► 71). You can retreat from the streets to green spaces such as the Parque Eduardo VII and the gardens around the castle (► 58–60), or the gardens of the Gulbenkian Museum (► 35). Browsing Lisbon's street markets and flea market (► 48) is excellent free entertainment. Last but not least, be sure to visit the Parque das Noções, the vast former Expo '98 site, where there are lots of free things to see and do.

WATCH YOUR STEP

Walking about is a must in Lisbon. As well as the *azulejos* that brighten the façades of numerous buildings (► 50), you will also see mosaics set into the pavements. Cobbled streets, steps and steep hills are hard on the feet, so wear comfortable shoes for your explorations.

Attractions for Children

PARQUE DAS NAÇÕES

Built for the '98 Expo, this site in east Lisbon has many attractions that will appeal to children. Apart from the Oceanário (► see this page), you can take a ride up the Vasco da Gama tower for excellent views over the city, River Tagus and Vasco da Gama Bridge or you can view the whole expo site from the Lisbon Cable Car 🔢 M2 ☎ 218 965 416 🕐 Tower daily; cable car Mon–Fri 11–7 🚇 Oriente

CASTELO DE BRINCAR

This tiny medieval castle-within-a-castle, in the Castelo de São Jorge, is full of slides, swings and ropes for children to play on.
🔢 J8, cIII ✉ Rua Costa do Castelo 🕐 Apr–end Sep daily 9–8/9; Oct–end Mar daily 9–6/7 🚌 37; tram 12, 28 ♿ Poor 🎫 Free

JARDIM ZOOLÓGICO DE LISBOA

Home to some 2,000 animals (350 species), Lisbon's zoo has long been underfunded with some enclosures appearing stark compared to some European counterparts. However, it claims to be Europe's best dolphinarium, and the dolphin shows and cable car appeal to children. The lovely garden setting is a pleasure to explore (► 59). Northwest of the city, it's best visited in conjunction with the nearby Palácio dos Marquêses de Fronteira (► 32, 59).
🔢 F4 ✉ Estrada de Benfica 158–160-Parque das Laranjeiras ☎ 217 232 900 🕐 Apr–end Sep daily 9–8; Oct–end Mar daily 9–6 🍴 Café 🚇 Sete Rios 🚌 16, 26, 31, 41, 54, 58 🎫 Expensive

OCEANÁRIO

Spectacularly designed by Peter Chermayeff, this is Europe's largest oceanarium. Opened in 1998, as part of Expo '98, it has water species from the five different oceans. The vast central tank is surrounded by four smaller tanks with two viewing levels.
🔢 M2 ✉ Praça das Nações ☎ 218 965 416 🕐 Daily 10–7 🚇 Oriente 🎫 Expensive

PLANETÁRIO CALOUSTE GULBENKIAN

Sponsored by the Gulbenkian Foundation, the Planetarium is an annex of the Museu de Marinha and has special children's shows.
🔢 B9 ✉ Praça do Império ☎ 213 620 002 🕐 Children's performances Wed–Thu 4pm, Sun 11am 🚇 Belém 🚌 27, 28, 29, 43, 49, 51; tram 15 🎫 Moderate

LISBON FOR CHILDREN

Sights such as the Torre de Belém (► 26), the children's museum in the Museu de Marinha (► 27), and Museu dos Coches (► 31) are likely to appeal to children. Other pastimes include a visit to the Feira Popular, the big funfair held in the north of the city centre (Mar–end Oct Mon–Fri 7pm–1.30am, Sat–Sun and public hols 3pm–1.30am); a ride on a tram; and boat trips (► 20, 61).

LISBON
where to...

Fine Dining

PRICES

Expect to pay per person for a meal excluding drinks:

€ under €15
€€ €15–25
€€€ over €25

COVER CHARGE, TAXES AND TIPS

Restaurants will often bring plates of starters such as bread, ham, cheeses and olives. These will be charged to your bill as *couvert* or cover charge unless you send them back. Very few people do this as they are great and unless you are in a very fancy restaurant they will make little difference to the final bill. Value added tax or IVA is added to restaurant bills at 8 per cent. Most bills say *IVA incluído* and already include this charge. Tips are welcomed and generally expected as a service charge is rarely included on the bill. Anything from 5 per cent is considered acceptable.

ANTÓNIO CLARA (€€€)

Polished wood, antiques and gilded mirrors set off the fine art nouveau decor of the 19th-century villa in which the restaurant is set. Dress up and revel in the ambience. Specialities include smoked swordfish and monkfish rice.

➕ H4 ✉ Avenida da República 38 ☎ 217 994 280 🕐 Mon–Sat lunch, dinner 🚇 Entrecampos

BACHUS (€€€)

A popular and stylish restaurant. Especially good are the mixed-grill Bachus, mountain goat and Bachus shrimp.

➕ H8; alII ✉ Largo da Trindade 9 ☎ 213 421 260 🕐 Tue–Fri lunch, dinner; Sat–Sun dinner only 🚌 58, 100

CASA DA COMIDA (€€€)

Among Lisbon's finest French-Portuguese restaurants, this is a good place to treat yourself, though it is well north-west of the city. The setting is wonderful—a former mansion in a little square. In summer you can eat outside.

➕ G7 ✉ Travessa das Amoireiras 1, off Rua Alexandre Herculano ☎ 213 859 386 🕐 Mon–Fri lunch, dinner; Sat dinner only 🚇 Rato 🚌 12, 18, 42, 51

COLARES VELHO (€€€)

If you are staying in the Sintra area and want to be sure of an excellent meal it is worth driving out to Colares (about 10 minutes drive to the west) to this excellent little restaurant. Try the monkfish in garlic and coriander sauce.

➕ Off map ✉ Largo Dr Carlos França, 1–4 Colares Sintra ☎ 219 292 406 🕐 Tue–Sun lunch, dinner

CONFRARIA AT YORK HOUSE (€€€)

Tucked away in a 17th-century former carmelite convent, this restaurant with its oasis-like courtyard has transformed its cuisine over the last few years. An extensive selection of traditional Portuguese dishes served with refined elegance.

➕ G8 ✉ Rue das Janelas Verdes 32 ☎ 213 962 435 🕐 Daily lunch, dinner 🚌 24, 40, 49, 60; tram 25

CONVENTUAL (€€–€€€)

This restaurant is finely decorated with antique and modern religious art and the famous Arraiolos carpets. Its religious theme continues in the names of its dishes: Pope of Avignon snails, and in its excellent *doces conventuais* tradition, sweet, eggy desserts originally made by nuns.

➕ G7–G8 ✉ Praça das Flores 45 ☎ 213 909 196 🕐 Tue–Sun lunch, dinner; Sat and Mon dinner only. Closed Aug 🚇 Rato, Avenida 🚌 100

O NOBRE (€€€)

A favourite among top politicians, this small and perhaps a little cramped establishment serves crab soup in its own shell, partridge stuffed with fois-gras and truffles cooked in port.

➕ C9 ✉ Rue das Mercês 71A/B ☎ 213 633 827 🕐 Daily lunch, dinner 🚌 14, 73

RESTAURANTE 33 (€€–€€€)

Close to many of the Avenida hotels and decorated in the style of an English hunting lodge, this restaurant includes such dishes as smoked salmon, lobster or pepper steak. Live piano music is often played while you eat.

✚ G7–G8 ✉ Rua Alexandre Herculano 33A ☎ 213 546 079 ⏱ Mon–Fri lunch, dinner; Sat dinner only 🚇 Marquês de Pombal 🚌 6, 74

SUA EXCÊLENCIA (€€–€€€)

Worth a visit if in the Lapa district. This restaurant is renowned for its innovative Angolan and Mozambican influenced Portuguese cuisine. Dishes include prawns in the Mozambique style, and an Angolan chicken dish. Booking essential.

✚ F8 ✉ Rua do Conde 34 ☎ 213 903 614 ⏱ Mon–Fri lunch, dinner; Sat–Sun dinner only. Closed Sep 🚌 27, 49; tram 25

TÁGIDE (€€€)

A very elegant restaurant up from the waterfront on a hilltop in the Chiado district. Tiled portraits of Portuguese queens punctuate the white-washed walls, and chandeliers hang above. Book early to secure a window table with lovely views over the port and city. Specialities include stuffed crab and cold orange and lemon soufflé with hot chocolate sauce.

✚ H8 ✉ Largo Académia Nacional de Belas Artes 18–20 ☎ 213 420 720 ⏱ Mon–Fri lunch, dinner 🚇 Baixa-Chiando 🚌 58, 100; tram 15, 28

TAVARES (€€€)

For years this glittering old-world establishment, founded as a café in 1784, had a reputation as the best of Lisbon's grand old restaurants. It still attracts politicians, diplomats and the literary set.

✚ H8; all ✉ Rua da Misericórdia 35–37 ☎ 213 421 112 ⏱ Mon–Sat lunch, dinner 🚇 Baixa-Chiado 🚋 Tram 15, 28

TERREIRO DO PAÇO (€€€)

This stylish spot has deservedly won plaudits from around the world as one of Europe's best restaurants. Creative, modern takes on traditional Portuguese food are served in a lovely brick-vaulted room.

✚ J8; bIV ✉ Alongside Lisboa Welcome Center, Praça do Comércio ☎ 210 312 850 ⏱ Mon–Sat lunch, dinner; Sun lunch only 🚇 Terréiro do Paço/Baixa-Chiado 🚌 All bus services to Praça do Comércio

VELA LATINA (€€€)

This light, airy and tastefully decorated restaurant boasting one of Lisbon's prime locations, stands on the waterfront beside the Torre de Belém. Don't get the restaurant confused with the popular self-service restaurant at the front of the complex. The chef mixes national and international cuisine.

✚ B10 ✉ Doca Bom Sucesso ☎ 213 017 118 ⏱ Mon–Sat lunch, dinner 🚌 29; tram 15

PRACTICALITIES

The Portuguese eat earlier than their Spanish neighbours. Lunch runs from around 12.30 to 2.30, while dinner lasts from 7.30 to 10.30. Some restaurants close all day Sunday and on Saturday lunchtime. Some also close on Wednesday. The menu in Portuguese is known as the *lista* or *ementa*. An *ementa turística* is not a tourist menu, but the menu of the day. There is usually a modest choice, and this menu often represents excellent value, especially in cheaper restaurants. The dish of the day is the *prato do dia*. Eating à la carte is *à lista*.

Most Fashionable

BOOKING

These are Lisbon's most hip restaurants. If you fancy joining the in crowd to see what all the fuss is about you must book early to avoid disappointment.

A CHARCUTARIA (€€–€€€)

Originally opening just for friends, demand grew and eventually this restaurant was opened to the public. It specialises in Alentejan dishes such as *açorda* (bread soup) and *migas* (fried bread and pork).
➕ H8 ✉ Rua do Alecrim 47 ☎ 213 423 845 🕐 Tue–Fri lunch, dinner; Sat–Sun dinner only 🚇 Cais do Sodré 🚌 58, 100

BICA DO SAPATO (€€–€€€)

Opened by the same owner as the ever popular Pap'Açorda (▶ 67), Bicado Sapato has become Lisbon's ultimate trendy restaurant. With its super modern interior of wood, glass and chrome, views over the river, and excellent sushi, it has been praised both at home and abroad.
➕ K8 ✉ Avenida Infante D Henrique, Armazem B ☎ 218 810 320 🕐 Tue–Sat lunch, dinner; Mon dinner only 🚌 9, 12, 46, 90

ESPAÇO LISBOA (€€–€€€)

It is worth eating here just for the architecture. In an old factory building, this huge restaurant is decorated with thousands of beautiful tiles. The menu focuses on Portuguese cooking.
➕ E9 ✉ Rua da Cozinha Económica 16 ☎ 213 610 212 🕐 Daily lunch, dinner 🚇 Alcântara–Cascais line from Cais do Sodré 🚌 38; tram 15, 18

LA VILLA (€€–€€€)

On the seafront at Estoril, this is an excellent choice if you want to get out of central Lisbon and dine above the beach. La Villa serves excellent sushi and there is an excellent nouvelle cuisine menu.
➕ Off map ✉ Praia do Estoril ☎ 214 680 033 🕐 Tue–Sun lunch, dinner 🚇 Estoril–Cascais line from Cais do Sodré

L'ENTRECOTE (€€)

The Chiado's smart set make for this traditional, but relaxed wood-panelled dining room for the faultless presentation and fine, upmarket French-influenced food. Steaks, as the name suggests, are a speciality. There is a good two-course set menu daily.
➕ H8; aIII ✉ Rua do Alecrim ☎ 213 428 343 🕐 Daily lunch, dinner 🚇 Baixa-Chiado 🚌 100, 58; tram 28

SOLAR DOS NUNES (€€)

This small restaurant serves game, including wild boar, partridge and hare in season. Also try the excellent value steaks.
➕ E9–8 ✉ Rua dos Lusiadas 68–72 ☎ 213 647 359/213 631 631 🕐 Mon–Sat lunch, dinner 🚌 22; tram 18, 15

XL (€€–€€€)

The ocre-painted walls, rustic furniture and antique curiosities give this extremely popular restaurant a cosy, homely feel. Camembert in bread crumbs with raspberry sauce and soufflés, are their forte.
➕ G8 ✉ Calçada da Estrela 57 ☎ 213 956 118 🕐 Mon–Sat dinner only 🚌 6, 13, 39, 49, 100; tram 28

Regional & Traditional

BOTA ALTA (€)

Attractive and rustic eaterie in the Bairro Alto. Big portions of traditional cooking draw the crowds.

✚ H7; alll ☎ Travessa da Queimada 35 ☎ 213 427 959 🕓 Mon–Fri lunch, dinner; Sat dinner only 🚇 Restauradores–Elevador da Glória or Baixa-Chiado 🚌 58; tram 28

CASA DO ALENTEJO (€€)

This restaurant in a 19th-century Franco-Arabic style building with wonderful tiles, is a celebration of the Alentejo region as much as of the Alentejan cuisine. There is often folk dancing on Saturdays.

✚ H7; all ✉ Praça Santo Antão-Rua das Portas de Santo Antão 58 ☎ 213 469 231 🕓 Daily lunch, dinner 🚇 Restauradores

LAUTASCO (€€)

This restaurant in the Alfama is popular with visitors and locals who come here not so much for the food, which is simple Portuguese fare, but for the delightful atmospheric courtyard.

✚ J8; clll ✉ Beco do Azinhal 7, off Rua de São Pedro-Largo Chafariz de Dentro ☎ 218 860 173 🕓 Mon–Sat lunch, dinner 🚌 104, 105

OLIVIER (€€)

A good choice if you want to try authentic national cooking. It's renowned for its Portuguese dishes such as *bacalhau* (salt cod) and *arroz de pato* (rice with duck).

✚ H8; all-lll ✉ Rua do Teixeira 35 ☎ 213 421 024 🕓 Mon–Fri

lunch, dinner; Sat dinner only. Closed Jul 🚇 Restauradores–Elevador da Glória 🚌 58, 100

O POLEIRO (€€)

Opened in 1985, this family-run restaurant serves traditional cusine in a simple but friendly environment.

✚ H4 ✉ Rua de Entrecampos 30-A ☎ 217 976 265 🕓 Mon–Fri lunch, dinner; Sat dinner only 🚇 Campo Pequeno/Entrecampos

PAP'AÇORDA (€€)

Trendy, predominantly young and arty clientele frequent this restaurant in a converted bakery. Try the *açorda* (bread soup).

✚ H8; alll ✉ Rua da Atalaia 57–9 ☎ 213 464 811 🕓 Tue–Sat lunch, two servings for dinner 8/8.30, 10/11.30 🚇 Baixa-Chiado 🚌 58, 100; tram 28

RESTAURANTE MALMEQUER-BEMMEQUER (€–€€)

A welcoming choice in an evocative street in the Alfama district. Plenty of basic Portuguese dishes.

✚ J8; clll ✉ Rua São Miguel 23–5, Largo de São Miguel ☎ 218 876 535 🕓 Tue–Sun lunch, dinner

VIA GRAÇA (€€–€€€)

This candlelit restaurant, with a romantic city view, is in the hilly reaches of the Graça district to the northeast of the Castelo de São Jorge. Cooking is traditional Portuguese.

✚ J7; cl ✉ Rua Damasceno Monteiro 98 ☎ 218 870 830 🕓 Mon–Fri lunch, dinner; Sat dinner only 🚇 Intendente 🚌 Tram 28

BASICS

Hors d'ouevres are *acepipes*. Breakfast is *pequeno almoço*, lunch *almoço*, and dinner *jantar*. Soups are typically cheap and filling as a first course. Meat (*carne*) and poultry (*aves*) are usually simply grilled or fried: roast or barbecued chicken is a particularly tasty Portuguese dish. Fish (*peixe*) and seafood (*mariscos*), though, are pre-eminent in Lisbon. Salt cod (*bacalhau*) and sardines (*sardinhas*) are virtually the national dishes. Vegetables are *legumes* and salad *salada*. Bread is *pão*.

TASCAS

Portugal's traditional eating haunts are known as *tascas* from the old word *tascar* to eat. A *tasca* serves no frills cuisine, just good honest traditional fare whose cooking and poorman's recipes uses bread, pork bits and whatever the earth provided for them. Portions are huge and prices very reasonable. This food is known as *comida regional*, though not relating to any particular region but rather to the country as a whole. It's the same as *comida tipic*, i.e. typically Portuguese.

Seafood

PORT

Port is a Douro region wine that is sweet because brandy has been added at a certain point to stop the grape sugar turning into alcohol. It may be red or white. Young red port, or *tinto*, is the most common, and is distinctive and very fruity. Reds are used to make blended ports, the blend comprising ports from different years, the quality depending on the wines used. Reds are also the basis of vintage, ruby and tawny ports (see panels below and opposite). White port, or *branco*, is sometimes fermented again to remove the sweetness. If chilled, this dry white port makes a delicious apéritif.

RUBY AND TAWNY

Ruby, or *tinto-aloirado*, is slightly older than *tinto*, hence its different colour, and will often be blended from a variety of more aged ports. Tawny, or *aloirado*, is made from port that has been aged for longer in the cask (usually at least seven years), a process which gives the port its distinctive golden-brown, or tawny colour.

CAIS DA RIBEIRA (€€€–€€)

In one of the many, now converted, warehouses along the dockside, this restaurant serves excellent fresh fish and seafood, and has fine views of the River Tagus.

H9; ✉ Armazem A-2, Cais do Sodré ☎ 213 423 611 ⏰ Mon–Fri lunch, dinner; Sat dinner only ⊕ Cais do Sodré 🚌 15, 18

CERVEJARIA PINÓQUIO (€€)

Established in the Baixa for over 30 years, this is a simple, no frills restaurant. Diners sit at long tables, service is quick but the fish is fresh, bought in daily from Setúbal; if the sea is rough supplies run low.

H7; all ✉ Praça dos Restauradores 79 ☎ 213 465 106 ⏰ Daily lunch, dinner 🚇 Restauradores

FAZ FIGURA (€€)

This restaurant provides excellent service and fine views over the River Tagus. The best on the menu includes *feijoada de marisco* (shellfish) and seafood *cataplana* (large round-bottomed copper dish).

K8 ✉ Rua do Paraiso 15B ☎ 218 868 981 ⏰ Mon–Sat dinner only 🚌 104, 105

FIDALGO (€€)

This popular rendezvous for media types is trendier than most of the Bairro Alto restaurants. Great fish.

H8; all ✉ Rua da Barroca 27 ☎ 213 422 900 ⏰ Mon–Sat lunch, dinner 🚇 Baixa-Chiado 🚌 58, 100; tram 28

GAMBRINUS (€€€)

This restaurant, just off the Rossio, is one of Lisbon's most expensive. The culinary emphasis is on fish and seafood. The setting is suitably formal, with leather chairs and beamed ceiling. Reservations are essential.

H7; all ✉ 25 Rua das Portas de Santo Antão 23 ☎ 213 421 466 ⏰ Daily lunch, dinner 🚇 Rossio/Restauradores

MERCADO DO PEIXE (€€€)

Perhaps one of Lisbon's more upmarket fish and seafood restaurants, it is well worth the trip out to Ajuda (just before Belém) to sample some of the best seafood in the city.

C8 ✉ Estrada de Casal Pedro Teixeira ☎ 213 623 140 ⏰ Tue–Sat lunch, dinner; Sun lunch only 🚌 27, 29; tram 18

SOLMAR (€€)

In this big, busy, down-to-earth place in the Baxia district seafood is the focus but there are also game dishes on the menu. Dine amid 1950s decor.

H7; all ✉ Rua das Portas de Sao Antão 108 ☎ 213 423 371 ⏰ Daily lunch, dinner 🚇 Restauradores 🚌 1, 2, 9, 11, 31, Avenida da Liberdade services

RIBADOURO (€-€€)

Eat informally at the bar or go downstairs to the main restaurant for a full meal. Excellent seafood.

H7 ✉ Corner of Rua do Salitre and Avenida da Liberdade 155 ☎ 213 549 411 ⏰ Daily lunch, dinner 🚇 Avenida 🚌 1, 2, 9, 11, 31 and all other Avenida da Liberdade services

International

ESCORIAL (€€-€€€)

A wood panelled dining room in the heart of the city with classic Spanish dishes such as roast kid or partridge casserole.

✚ H7; all ✉ Rua das Portas de Santo Antão 47 ☎ 213 464 429 🕐 Daily lunch, dinner 🚇 Restauradores

COMIDA DE SANTO (€€)

This lively Brazilian restaurant is known for its powerful cocktails and South American-influenced Portuguese dishes. Try the delicious *feijoada* (bean stew).

✚ G7 ✉ Calçada Engenheiro Miguel Pais 39, off Rua da Escola Politécnica ☎ 213 963 339 🕐 Daily lunch, dinner 🚍 58,100

DELHI PALACE (€€)

This popular, Indian-owned restaurant just west of the cathedral offers a mixture of Indian and Italian food, though it is recommended more for its curries than its pasta.

✚ J8; clII ✉ Rua da Padaria 18–20 ☎ 218 884 203 🕐 Tue–Sun lunch, dinner 🚇 Terréiro do Paço 🚍 37; tram 12, 28

MASSIMA CULPA (€€)

A spaghetti house with a wide range of Italian pasta and a young, lively atmosphere. Don't miss its champagne sangria.

✚ H8; alII ✉ Rua da Atalaia 35/37 ☎ 213 420 121 🕐 Thu–Tue dinner only 🚍 58, 100; tram 28

MEZZALUNA (€€)

An Italian restaurant catering for a slightly older, quieter crowd.

✚ G6 ✉ Rua Artilharia Um 16 ☎ 213 879 944 🕐 Mon–Fri lunch, dinner; Sat dinner only 🚇 Marqués de Pombal 🚍 11, 23, 48, 53

O CANTINHO DO AZIZ (€)

Informal and rather rough and ready, this is a great place to sample spicy Mozambique and Angolan cooking. A little hard to find: it is tucked away in the northwest corner of the Alfama district.

✚ J8; bII ✉ Rua de São Lourenço 3–5 ☎ 218 876 472 🕐 Mon–Sat lunch, dinner 🚇 Rossio/Martim Moniz

PICANHA (€€)

Excellent Brazilian grilled meats, *farofa* (manioc), *feijão* (beans) and other Brazilian delights. Try the *caipirinhas*, alcoholic lemon punches.

✚ G9–10 ✉ Rua das Janelas Verdes 96 ☎ 213 975 401 🕐 Mon–Fri lunch, dinner; Sat–Sun dinner only 🚍 27, 40, 49, 60; tram 25

ÚLTIMO TANGO (€-€€)

In the Bairro Alto, this Argentinian restaurant serves excellent steaks and a fine selection of Argentinian wines.

✚ H8, alII ✉ Rua Diário de Noticias 62 ☎ 213 420 341 🕐 Mon–Sat lunch, dinner 🚍 58, 100; tram 28

VELHA GÔA (€€)

Tasty Goanese cuisine, with mild to flaming hot curries; try the prawn chicken or Madrasta.

✚ F7 ✉ Rua Tomás da Anunciação 41 ☎ 213 900 446 🕐 Mon–Fri lunch, dinner; Sat dinner only 🚍 74, tram 25, 28

COLONIAL INFLUENCE

Colonial days may be long gone but their inheritance lives on especially in Portugal's cuisine. As the Portuguese returned from the ex-colonies they brought with them such dishes as *moamba* from Angola, *cachupa* from Caboverde, and the typical tiger prawns grilled in *piri-piri* sauce from Mozambique. From Goa came the *chamuças* and curries and from Brazil the roast meats of the *picanha* and the famous bean feast known as *feijoada Brazilieira*.

All these and many more can now be found around the city, both in their own typical restaurants and dotted through the menus of traditionally Portuguese establishments, often opened by those who spent years abroad.

Light Meals

HALF PORTIONS

Servings tend to be generous in Portugal, and many soups and starters are rich and filling enough to be meals in themselves. If you can't manage whole portions, ask if you can have a half portion, or share one serving between two—many restaurants are happy to serve smaller portions, especially those in the lower price range, and some even list half portions on the menu.

WITH CHILDREN

Eating out with children should not be a problem—it is common to see even very young children out with their parents late at night. Restaurants are welcoming and serve half portions, or are happy to let young children share their parents' meals.

CERVEJARIAS

Cervejarias or beer houses are a great option when looking for a quick, light meal. With a limited menu of steaks and chips, prawns and of course beer, these are Portugal's equivalent of fast food restaurants, serving food into the early hours.

ACADÉMICA (€)

In good weather you can eat snacks or light meals (or simply enjoy a drink) outdoors on one of the city's loveliest squares, in the shadow of the ruined Carmo church.
➕ H8; alll ✉ Largo do Carmo 1–3 ☎ 213 469 092 🕐 Daily 7am–midnight 🚇 Baix-Chiado 🚌 58, 100; tram 28; Elevador de Santa Justa

ALFAIA (€)

A busy and popular restaurant, especially for lunch. You need search no further for a reasonably priced meal in a typical Bairro Alto establishment.
➕ H8; alll ✉ Travessa da Queimada 18–24 ☎ 213 461 232 🕐 Tue–Sat, lunch, dinner; Mon lunch only 🚌 Restauradores

BONJARDIM (€–€€)

This Lisbon institution, with three outlets on the same street, appeals to all tastes and budgets. The downstairs dining room is lined with tiles and there are wooden beams upstairs.
➕ H7; all ✉ Travessa de Santo Antão 10–11 ☎ 213 427 424 or 213 424 389 🕐 Daily lunch, dinner 🚌 Restauradores

CAFÉ NO CHIADO (€–€€)

A restored 18th-century building filled with modern furnishings serving steak and chips to a young, artistic crowd.
➕ H8; all ✉ Largo do Picadeiro 10–12 ☎ 213 460 501 🕐 Daily lunch, dinner 🚇 Baixa-Chiado 🚌 58, 100

CASA FAZ FRIO (€)

On the northern edge of the Bairro Alto, this is one of Lisbon's lovelier and more traditional restaurants. Known for its low prices and good seafood.
➕ H7 ✉ Rua Dom Pedro V 96 ☎ 213 461 860 🕐 Daily lunch, dinner 🚇 Restauradores–Elevador da Glória 🚌 58, 100

CERVEJARIA TRINDADE (€–€€)

This large beer hall and azulejo-lined restaurant, in a former convent in the Chiado, is one of the city's oldest eating places, in business since 1836. The food is nothing special, but the place is a classic, and a fun spot.
➕ H8; alll ✉ Rua Nova da Trindade 20b ☎ 213 423 506 🕐 Mon–Sat 8pm–late 🚇 Baixa-Chiado 🚌 20, 24, 100; tram 28, 58

ENOTECA (€€)

In the beautiful 18th-century building known as the Chafariz do Vinho, it's an excellent place for a tapas style plate of ham, spicey sausage and cheeses, plus a glass of wine.
➕ H7 ✉ Rua da Mãe d' Água à Praça da Alegria ☎ 213 422 079 🕐 Tue–Sun dinner only from 6pm 🚇 Restauradores–Elevador da Glória 🚌 58, 100

PORTUGÁLIA RIO (€€)

One of the several Portugália cervejarias around the city—this one enjoys the best location. A limited selection of good, fast food; open until late.
➕ H9 ✉ Cintura do Porto de Lisboa, Armazem 63 ☎ 213 422 138 🕐 Daily lunch, dinner 🚇 Cais do Sodré 🚌 14, 28, 40, 43

Cafés and *Pastelarias*

ANTIGA CASA DOS PASTÉIS DE BELÉM

This old café and pastry shop in Belém is renowned for its cakes, particularly the distinctive *pastéis de Belém*, tiny flaky tarts filled with custard.

⊞ C9 ⊠ Rua de Belém 84–90 ☎ 213 637 423 ⊟ 27, 28, 29, 43, 49, 51; tram 15

CAFÉ A BRASILEIRA

The most famous of Lisbon's venerable coffee-houses at the heart of the fashionable Chiado district. A favoured retreat for writers and artists, notably the poet Fernando Pessoa, a statue of whom sits outside on the pavement. It has plenty of tables outdoors, and remains open until late, when the atmosphere is less sedate.

⊞ H8; alll ⊠ Rua Garrett 120 ☎ 213 469 541 ⧉ Baixa-Chiado ⊟ 58,100; tram 28

CAFÉ CERCA MOURA

Situated close to the Miradouro Santa Luzia in the Largo das Portas do Sol, this café has fine views of the River Tagus and a good selection of snacks and drinks.

⊞ J8; Clll ⊠ Largo das Portas do Sol 4 ☎ 218 874 859

CAFÉ MARTINHO DA ARCADA

Like the Nicola (see below) on the Rossio and A Brasileira (see above) in the Chiado, this old coffee-house, founded in 1782, was a haunt of Lisbon's 19th-century literati. The adjoining restaurant is expensive, but the bar is still a good spot for coffee and snacks. Wood-panelled counter.

⊞ J8; blV ⊠ Praça do Comércio 3 ☎ 218 866 213 ⧉ Rossio ⊟ 11, 13, 81 and all services to Praça do Comércio; tram 15, 18, 25

CAFÉ NICOLA

This lovely old place dating from 1777 was a haunt for Lisbon's literary set in the 19th century and is now one of the city's most popular cafés—it can be hard to find a table.

⊞ H8; alll ⊠ Rua Primeiro de Dezembro; entrance also at Praça Dom Pedro IV 24 (Rossio) ☎ 213 460 579 ⧉ Rossio

CASA CHINEZA

Join locals for a mid-morning stand-up snack in this beautifully decorated traditional *pastelaria* in the heart of the Baixa.

⊞ J8; blll ⊠ Rua da Aurea 274–78 ☎ 213 423 680 ⧉ Baixa-Chiado ⊟ All Avenida da Liberdade services

PASTELARIA BÉNARD

One of Lisbon's finest and long-established cafés and pastry shops; the desserts are particularly famous. On the Chiado's most fashionable street.

⊞ H8; alll ⊠ Rua Garrett 104–106 ☎ 213 473 133 ⧉ Baixa-Chiado

PASTELARIA SUIÇA

This café and pastry shop on Lisbon's main square competes with the Café Nicola (see above) opposite. Both have large and busy terraces.

⊞ H8; alll ⊠ Praça Dom Pedro IV 96–100 ☎ 213 214 090 ⧉ Rossio

PASTELARIAS

If you are looking for a light meal in stylish surroundings, then it is worth considering traditional cafés and pastry shops such as Pastelaria Bénard, Café A Brasileira and others (► this page). Best known as places for coffee and a pastry, they usually serve snacks and sandwiches too, and may stay open well into the evening.

DRINKS

Coffee in Portugal is *café*. For a small espresso-type shot ask for *um café* or *uma bica*, if you want a dash of milk added ask for *um garoto*. A longer, milkier coffee is *um galão*, but is usually more milk than coffee. For a strong large coffee, ask for a double espresso (*um café duplo*) with milk (*um pouco de leite*). Tea (*chá*) is very popular, and is served either plain, with milk (*com leite*) or with lemon (*um chá de limão*). The most popular yellow beer (*cerveja*) is the Lisbon-brewed Sagres; Sagres Preta is a British-style brown beer. Beer comes in bottles or in measures of a half-litre (*uma caneca*) or quarter-litre in a tall slim glass (*um imperial*). Mineral water is *água mineral*, either fizzy (*com gás*) or still (*sem gás*).

71

Shopping Districts & Malls

MALLS

AMOREIRAS

Lisbon's first mall is in the Torres das Amoreiras in the north of the city. This distinctive and very visible building was designed by Tomás Taveira, one of Portugal's leading architects. It contains a hotel, ten cinemas, over 70 cafés and restaurants, and more than 350 shops. Most stay open until late, seven days a week (Sundays are particularly busy).
➕ F7 ✉ Avenida Engenheiro Duarte Pacheco ☎ 213 810 200 🚌 15, 23, 48, 53, 58, 78

COLOMBO

For a post-modern shopping experience join the Lisboetans at the massive Colombo shopping mall opposite the Benfica football stadium in the north of the city. At the time of completion this mall claimed to be Iberia's largest with three floors of shops, a hypermarket, restaurants, cinemas and a fun park with go-carts and an indoor roller coaster.
➕ D3 ✉ Avenida do Colégio Militar ☎ 217 113 600; www.colombo.pt 🚇 Colégio Militar

VASCO DA GAMA

This is Lisbon's newest shopping mall opened in 1999 at the Expo '98 site in the east of the city. It contains all the usual fashion labels, restaurants and a cinema complex.
➕ M4 ✉ Avenida Dom João II ☎ 218 930 600 🚇 Oriente

DISTRICTS

AVENIDA DA LIBERDADE

Lisbon's main avenue has long been home to many exclusive and stylish clothes stores. This can be a pleasant place to shop while also taking in the beautiful architecture and pavement mosaics. Gift and craft shops at the Rossio end.
➕ H6–H7 🚇 Marquês de Pombal/Avenida/Restauradores 🚌 All Avenida Liberdade services

AVENIDA DE ROMA

Although not as convenient as the purpose built malls, this busy road has plenty of variety; as well as major labels there are fashion stores selling shoes, handbags and clothes.
➕ H3–J4 🚇 Roma 🚌 7, 33 and many others

BAIRRO ALTO (► 37)

This district is gaining a reputation as a place to buy clothes, furniture and household goods.
➕ H8 🚇 Baixa-Chiado

BAIXA (► 42)

Many traditional trades still flourish in this area at the heart of the city. In recent years several fashion chains have opened shops here adding new life to the area.
➕ J8; bIII 🚇 Baixa-Chiado

CHIADO (► 39)

Chiado is Lisbon's top shopping district, its streets dotted with expensive shoe shops and designer clothes shops.
➕ H8; aIII 🚇 Baixa-Chiado

Food & Drink

A CARIOCA

From behind a lovely art nouveau shopfront in the Bairro Alto, A Carioca has been providing superb tea and coffee to Lisbon since 1937. The blends come from around the world.
⊞ JH8; alll ✉ Rua da Misericórdia 9 ☎ 213 420 377 Ⓜ Baixa-Chiado 🚌 20, 24, 100; tram 28

CASA MACÁRIO

Casa Macário in Rua Augusta has bottles of port dating back to 1875 and beyond at predictably high prices. You may not want to spend so much, but port and Madeira are the obvious drinks to take home as a souvenir.
⊞ J4; blll ✉ Rua Augusta 272–276 ☎ 213 420 377

CHÁ CASA PEREIRA

This family-run shop, founded in 1930, sells teas and coffees blended and ground to your own taste. Other tempting items include vintage port and mouthwatering chocolates.
⊞ H8; alll ✉ Rua Garrett 38 ☎ 213 426 694 Ⓜ Baixa-Chiado 🚌 20, 24, 100; tram 28

COISAS DO ARCO DO VINHO

This big wine showroom inside the Centro Cultural de Belém organises gastronomy sessions and other wine related events, and sells a competently chosen range of wines.
⊞ B10 ✉ Centro Cultural de Belém, Praça do Império ☎ 213 642 031; www.coisasdoarcodo vinho.ot Ⓜ Belém (Cascais line from Cais do Sodré) 🚌 27, 28, 29, 43, 49, 51; tram 15

ESPÍRITO DO VINHO

This is a wine lovers paradise. They sell the finest wines from Portugal and abroad.
⊞ G8 ✉ Rua Borges Carneiro 38 ☎ 213 859 078 🚌 13, 27

MANUEL TAVARES

For glorious food head to this shop in the Baxia, an institution for over 100 years.
⊞ J8; blll ✉ Rua da Betesga 1A/B ☎ 213 424 209 Ⓜ Rossio

O CELEIRO

O Celeiro sells natural foods, medicines, vitamins and cosmetics.
⊞ H8; alll ✉ Loja 1, Rua 1 de Dezembro 65 ☎ 213 422 463 Ⓜ Rossio

PANIFICAÇÃO MECÂNICA

There are many good bakeries around town, but if you are in the area of Campo de Ourique this shop has a huge selection of bread, cakes and pastries.
⊞ G8 ✉ Rua Silva Carvalho, 209–223 Ⓜ Rato 🚌 58, 74

WINE SHOPS

CO-OPERATIVE WINE SHOP
⊞ H8; alll; IV ✉ Rua do Alecrim 24, Chiado ☎ 213 423 590

NAPOLEÃO IN THE BAIXA
⊞ J8; blll ✉ Rua dos Fanqueiros 70 ☎ 218 861 108

ULITRO IN THE BAIRRO ALTO
⊞ H8; alll ✉ Rua da Barroca ☎ 213 425 213

VINTAGE PORT

Vintage port–the best port–is made from the grapes of one year only, and then only if that year's harvest has been specially declared of vintage quality. It is bottled after two to four years in the cask and then ages for at least ten years in the bottle. Since 1974 a port must have been bottled in Portugal to be labelled a vintage. Late-bottled port (LBV) is a port that is not quite up to vintage standard, but is still deemed good enough to mature in the bottle rather than the cask. Typically it is bottled after about four to six years. Crucially, port that ages in the bottle matures by reduction, turning a deep-red. Port which ages in the cask matures through oxidation, and turns towards amber. The longer in the cask, the lighter the shade.

Fashion, Leather & Footwear

FASHION CAPITAL

Fashion designers are a relatively recent phenomenon in Lisbon (since the mid-1980s), but now with the help of such fashion events as the yearly *Moda Lisboa*, usually held in April, and *Vestir o Milenio* (Dressing the Millennum) in June, national designers are getting the publicity they deserve. From established names such as Fátima Lopes and Ana Salazar to the more recent talent of Maria Gambina and José António Tenente, Portuguese creations can now be found in shops and on the catwalks of Paris, London and Barcelona.

ANA SALAZAR

Ana Salazar is perhaps the best-known Portuguese fashion designer on the international stage. She is known primarily for her daring designs, and for special stretch fabrics. Currently she has two outlets in the city. The most central is the shop on Rua do Carmo, in the Chiado.

H8; a–bIII ✉ Rua do Carmo 87 ☎ 213 472 289 🚇 Rossio 🚌 2, 31, 36, 41 H3–J4 ✉ Avenida de Roma 16e ☎ 218 486 799 🚇 Roma

CASA DO TURISTA

This shop does sell a selection of tacky souvenirs but it also has some tasteful regional clothing and accessories including sweaters from Póvoa do Varzim near Oporto and scarves from the Minho.

H7; all ✉ Avenida da Liberdade 159 ☎ 213 151 558 🚇 Rossio/Avenida

COELHO PELEIRO

Excellent for leather belts, they can make leather backed fabric belts to order from your own material in its workshop next door. It also sells a variety of accessories.

J8; bIII ✉ Rua da Conceição 85 ☎ 213 425 770 🚇 Baixa-Chiado

ELDORADO

Second-hand vintage clothing, mainly from the 1950s, 60s and 70s. It also sells records.

H8; all ✉ Rua do Norte 23 ☎ 213 423 935 🚇 Baixa-Chiado

FÁTIMA LOPES

A degree of daring would be required in order to wear Fátima Lopes' creations, but this designer has become a regular on the Portuguese catwalks. Another branch on the Avenida de Roma.

H8; all ✉ Rua da Atalaia 36 ☎ 213 240 540 🚇 Baixa-Chiado 🚌 58, 100; tram 28

GALEÃO

In the heart of the Baixa, Galeão has a fine collection of leather belts and luggage.

J8; bIII ✉ Rua Augusta 190 ☎ 213 470 886 🚇 Baixa-Chiado

JOSÉ ANTÓNIO TENENTE

José António Tenente opened his shop on Rua do Carmo in 1990. His exclusive lines are considered more conservative than other Barrio Alto boutiques.

H8; all ✉ Travessa do Carmo 8 ☎ 213 422 560 🚇 Baixa-Chiado

LUVARIA ULISSES

This tiny shop is a treasure trove of gloves in every material imaginable, including silk, satin, lace, leather and cotton.

H8; all ✉ Rua do Carmo 87–A ☎ 213 420 295 🚇 Rossio

SAPATEIRO LISBOENSE

This shop is just one of the many in the Baixa selling quality shoes, bags, suitcases and belts.

J8; bIII ✉ Rua Augusta 202–204 ☎ 213 426 712 🚇 Baixa-Chiado

Art, Maps, Books & Music

BRITÂNICA

If you find you need more reading material while in Lisbon, this bookshop in the Rato sells in books in the English language.

⊞ H7 ⊠ Rua de São Marçal 8 ☎ 213 428 472 🚊 58

FNAC

One of the many foreign retail chains to open in Lisbon over the past few years, FNAC has the most comprehensive selection of books (including foreign language sections), music and maps.

⊞ D3 ⊠ Shop No. A–103, Colombo Shopping Mall ☎ 217 114 237; ww.fnac.pt 🚇 Colégio Militar
⊞ H8; bIII ⊠ Rua Nova do Almada 104–110 ☎ 213 221 800 🚇 Baixa-Chiado

GALERIA III

By far the most famous commercial art gallery in Lisbon, the outlying Galleria III has been in business since 1964. It shows and sells only the very best and most expensive works by Portuguese artists, and so is for serious buyers and browsers only. Art enthusiasts who might invest in its postcards, art books and cheaper prints, drawings and etchings.

⊞ H4 ⊠ Campo Grande 111–113 ☎ 217 977 418 🚇 Entrecampos 🚌 36a, 47

GALERIA SESIMBRA

Near the Ritz Hotel, this gallery displays the finest of Portuguese painting, sculpture and ceramics along with several foreign artists now resident in Portugal. It is best known for its hand-made Agulha tapestries.

⊞ G6 ⊠ Rua do Castilho ☎ 213 870 291 🚇 Marquês de Pombal

LIVRARIA BUCHHOLZ

This pleasantly jumbled three-floor shop not only sells a range of English-language books (as well as an excellent range of Portuguese titles), but also is one of the few outlets to sell Portuguese folk and other ethnic music.

⊞ H7 ⊠ Rua Duque de Palmela 4 ☎ 213 170 580 🚇 Marquês de Pombal

TABACARIA MÓNACO

This tiny newsagent and tobacconist is a Lisbon landmark. Founded in 1893, it preserves a wonderful art nouveau ambience, with a lovely tiled and painted interior. It is also a good place to come for maps, guides and foreign newspapers and magazines.

⊞ H8–J8; bII–bIII ⊠ Praça Dom Pedro IV 21 (Rossio) ☎ 213 468 191 🕔 Daily 9–7.30 🚇 Rossio 🚌 1, 2, 11 and all other services to the Rossio ❓ No credit cards

VALENTIM DE CARVALHO

Fado is not to all tastes, but if you want an authentic souvenir of your visit to Lisbon then this is the place to come. Also contemporary Portuguese pop and rock.

⊞ H8–J8; bII–bIII ⊠ Edifício Granella, Rua do Carmo 28 ☎ 214 401 000 🚇 Baixa-Chiado 🚌 1, 2, 11 and all other services to the Rossio

Crafts, Gifts & Souvenirs

BARCELOS COCKS

Although originally from Barcelos in the north, it's hard to avoid the ubiquitous Barcelos Cock painted pottery and wooden models that assault you from every souvenier shop and stall, especially since adapted by the tourist authority as their emblem. The cock's story is simple and reports a tale told across the Iberian peninsula. A pilgrim heading for Santiago de Compostela was unjustly accused of theft on leaving Barcelos. Despite pleading innocence he was found guilty and sentenced to death. Looking at the roast cockerel served for the judges dinner, he invoked the help of St. James, saying that if he were innocent the dead cock would crow. This promptly did and the man was released.

ARTESANATO REGIONAL PORTUGUÊS

One of the oldest handicraft shops in Lisbon (opened 1960s) with a wide assortment of genuine handmade articles displayed in 300m of showrooms a block down from the Post Office building.

⊕ H7; all ⊠ Praça dos Restauradores 64 ☎ 213 477 875 🚇 Restauradores

CASA ALVES

Selling items worked in copper including shallow round-bottomed copper dishes known as *cataplanas*, in which the rich fish and seafood dish from which it takes its name is served.

⊕ J8; blll ⊠ Rua Augusta 51 ☎ 213 475 429 🚇 Baixa-Chiado

CASA DAS CORTIÇAS

Cork (*cortiças*) is one of Portugal's most distinctive exports—it controls a vast proportion of the world's trade in the commodity. This singular little shop sells all sorts of objects—many rather unlikely—fashioned from the material, providing a uniquely Portuguese gift or souvenir to take home.

⊕ G7–H7 ⊠ Rua da Escola Politécnica 4–6 ☎ 213 425 858 🚌 58

CASA DE BORDADOS DE MADEIRA

Inside the Avenida Palace hotel, this shop sells embroideries from Viana do Castelo and Madeira (expensive) and the famous fishermen's sweaters from Póvoa do Varzim.

⊕ H8; alll ⊠ Rua 1 de Dezembro 135–139 ☎ 213 421 447 🚇 Restauradores 🚌 1, 2, 36, 44 or any of Avenida de Liberdade services

CASA MACIEL

Lisbon is full of long-established shops: this one was founded in 1810, and has grown from a small metal-working factory into an award-winning outlet for all manner of beautifully crafted work in metal. Pieces can be made to individual designs if required.

⊕ H8; all–alll ⊠ Rua da Misericórdia 63–5 ☎ 213 422 451 🚇 Rossio 🚌 58, 100; tram 28

CUSTÓDIO CARDOSO PEREIRA

Shop selling beautiful 12-stringed guitars used to accompany the fado.

⊕ H8; alll ⊠ Largo do Chiado 20 ☎ 213 224 180 🚇 Baixa-Chiado

FÁBRICA DE CÉRAMICA VIÚVA LAMEGO

Not as venerable as the Fábrica Sant'Anna (see below), this factory nonetheless dates back to 1879. The factory shop is adorned with tiles on its exterior, and sells mainly copies of traditional designs, together with a small selection of pottery. It will also design and make tiles to order.

⊕ J7; bl ⊠ Largo do Intendente Pina Manique 25 ☎ 218 852 402; www.viuvalamego.com 🚇 Intendente 🚌 7, 8, 40; tram 17, 28

FÁBRICA SANT'ANNA

This historic company has been Portugal's leading producer of *azulejos*, or decorated tiles, since 1741. The Rua do Alecrim address is the shop for its beautifully decorated products, many of which are based on traditional designs. It is also possible to visit the main factory by prior arrangement.

➕ H8 ✉ Rua do Alecrim 95–7 ☎ 213 422 537 🚌 58, 100; tram 28. Factory
➕ D9 ✉ Calçada da Boa Hora 96 ☎ 213 638 292

JOALHARIA DO CARMO

In business for almost a century, Joalharia do Carmo has few rivals when it comes to gold and silver filigree jewellery. It sells a wide variety of products, virtually all of them handmade.

➕ H8; alll–blll ✉ Rua do Carmo 87b ☎ 213 424 200 🚇 Rossio 🚌 21, 31, 36, 41, all services to Rossio

KÁ

Selling modern pieces by up-and-coming artists in papier-maché, glass, metal, stone and wood. In the Centro Cultural de Belém complex.

➕ B10 ✉ Centro Cultural de Belém, Praça do Império ☎ 213 612 400 🚇 Belém (Cascais line from Cais do Sodré) 🚌 27, 28, 29, 43, 49, 51; tram 15

PAÍS EM LISBOA

Hidden in the narrow streets of the Bairro Alto, this shop sells in dolls dressed in traditional costume. It also has a fine selection of linen.

➕ H8 ✉ Rua de Teixeira 25 🚇 Restauradores–Elevadar da Gloria 🚌 58

SANTOS OFICIOS

This handicraft shop founded in 1995 is inside a restored 18th-century stable. It sells handmade products from around the country including ceramics, linens and sheepskin slippers.

➕ J8; blll ✉ Rua da Madalena 87 ☎ 218 872 031 🚇 Baixa-Chiado 🚌 7, 40; trams 15

SARMENTO

The family-run firm of Sarmento has been Lisbon's most prestigious jeweller for almost a hundred years. The gold, silverware and filigree here are some of the most exquisite in Portugal.

➕ H8; blll ✉ Rua Áurea (Rua do Ouro) 251 ☎ 213 426 774 🚇 Baixa-Chiado 🚋 Tram 28

TABACARIA A PHOENIX LTD

Found in the Rossio, this *tabacaria* (tobacconists) does a line in regional baskets, which can make ideal gifts. It also sells guide books, lighters and other gift items.

➕ H8; blll ✉ Praça Dom Pedro IV 40 ☎ 213 225 769 🚇 Rossio 🚌 14, 37, 43, 59 or any other Rossio service

VIÚVA LAMEGO

This is one of the top shops in Lisbon for beautiful tiles, including faïence and copies of traditional designs. Order your own design.

➕ H8; alll ✉ Calçada do Sacramento 29 ☎ 213 469 692 🚇 Baixa-Chiado

CASA BATALHA

At the time of the great Chiado fire (1988), Casa Batalha had already been serving its customers on Rua Nova do Almada for 350 years. The tradition of selling costume jewellery and accessories has been passed down through seven generations since 1635. It is now back trading in the heart of Lisbon at its age old location.

✉ Rua Nova do Almado, 75–77 🚇 Baixa-Chiado

TILES GALORE

Azulejos have been decorating not only palaces, churches, chapels and public buildings for centuries but also the homes of Portugal, helping to waterproof against the winter rains. Very popular as souvenirs, you can find a vast array of fine hand-painted, antique and contemporary tiles to give to your friends or adorn your home.

For the Home

ARRAIOLOS CARPETS

The attractive little town of Arraiolos lies 150km east of Lisbon and has been famous for centuries for its superlative hand-woven carpets. The patterns originally owed much to Moorish and Persian designs, but these days, while still beautiful, they tend to be less complex. Prices are fairly high whether buying one in Lisbon or Arraiolos.

ARQUITECTÓNICA

This is a good place to go if looking for avant-garde designer furniture and furnishings.

✚ H7; ✉ Rua da Escola Politécnica 94 ☎ 213 979 605 ⓠ Rato 🚌 58, 100

A TRINIDADE

As well as having a fine collection of antique porcelain and religious art this antique shop on the Rua do Alecrim specialises in antique furniture.

✚ H8; alll ✉ Rua do Alecrim 79–81 ☎ 213 424 660 ⓠ Baixa-Chiado 🚌 58, 100

CASA DAS VELAS DO LORETO

This venerable shop in the Bairro Alto has been in the business of producing candles of all shapes and sizes for over 200 years.

✚ H8; alll ✉ Rua do Loreto 53 ☎ 213 425 387 ⓠ Restauradores

CASA REGIONAL DA ILHA VERDE

Selling all manner of craft items from the Ilha Verde (Green Island), more commonly known as San Miguel in the Azores. Fabrics, linens and embroidery are their forte. Much of the work is based on age-old designs.

✚ H7 ✉ Rua Paiva de Andrade 4 ☎ 213 425 974 ⓠ Restauradores 🚌 1, 2, 36, 44 and other Avenida do Liberdade services

DEPOSITO DA MARINHA GRANDE

These no-nonsense Bairro Alto shops are outlets for Marinha Grande's own reasonably priced glass and china. The firm is long established, and its Atlantis glass is particularly well known in Portugal.

✚ G7–G8 ✉ Rua de São Bento 234–242 ☎ 213 963 234 ⓠ Rato 🚌 6 49 Also at ✚ G7–G8 ✉ Rua de São Bento 418–420 ☎ 213 963 096 ⓠ Rato 🚌 6, 49

EL CORTE INGLÉS

The vast ninth-floor department store has numerous good-quality household items, as well as a wide range of other general goods. The basement level is devoted to food, with delis, bakers and other gastronomic outlets, while there are cafés and restaurants on the upper level.

✚ G5 ✉ Avenida António de Aguiar ☎ 213 711 700; www.elcorteingles.pt ⓠ São Sebastião 🚌 16, 26, 31 and all services to Avenida António Augusto de Aguiar

MADEIRA HOUSE

This shop sells high quality cottons, linens and gift items from the island of Madeira. It has two outlets, one in the Baixa and the other on the Avenida da Liberdade.

✚ J8; blll ✉ Rua Augusta 131–135 ☎ 213 426 813 ⓠ Rossio/Baixa-Chiado 🚌 All services to Praça do Comécio or Rossio

M. MURTEIRA

If walking up to the Castelo de São Jorge you will probably pass this charming antiques shop selling curiosities from the 18–19th century. Everything from bed

heads to bird cages.
 J8; clll ✉ Rua Augusto Rosa 19–21 ☎ 218 863 851 🚇 37; tram 28

OLARIA DO DESTERRO

Just off the Rua da Palma Almirante Reis is this 150-year-old shop selling traditional earthenware pieces such as plates and casseroles.
🚉 J7; bl ✉ Rua Nova do Desterro 14 ☎ 218 850 013 🚇 Martim Moniz/Intendente 🚌 7, 8, 40; tram 17, 28

PRÍNCIPE REAL

This prestigious firm produces and sells some of the loveliest table linens, cottons and other fabrics in the city. Royalty and all manner of rich and famous clients have patronised the shop over the years. Sheets and tablecloths are good buys, and prices are not as outrageous as you might expect.
🚉 G7–H7 ✉ Rua da Escola Politécnica 12–14 ☎ 213 465 945 🚌 58, 100

RETROSARIA E ESTABELECIMENTOS NARDO

If you are looking for anything related to haberdashery then try this shop in the Baixa, which has a wide selection of buttons, ribbons, cords and threads.
🚉 J8; blll ✉ Rua da Conceição 62–64 ☎ 213 421 350 🚇 Baixa-Chiado

SOLAR

Rua Dom Pedro V is where you will find many of the cities best antique shops. This particular one is good for original tiles

taken from manor houses and historic buildings dating back to the 15th century. It also has a good selection of pewter ware and furniture.
🚉 H7 ✉ Rua Dom Pedro V 68–70 ☎ 213 465 522 🚇 Restauradores 🚌 58,100

TERESA ALECRIM

This shop is named after its owner who produces fine high quality embroideries created in plain or patterned cotton in the Laura Ashley style. Pillowcases, sheets, towels and covers are but a few items she offers.
🚉 H8; blll ✉ Rua Nova do Almada 76 ☎ 213 421 831 🚇 Baixa-Chiado 🚌 2; tram 28
Also at ✉ Amoreiras Complex, Shop No.1116 ✉ Avenida da Roma 68

VISTA ALEGRE

In business since 1824, this prestigious firm is renowned in Portugal and beyond for its exquisite porcelain dinner sets and china. It supplied Portuguese royalty until 1910, and today still supplies china to many of the royal families of Europe. It also sells cheaper but nonetheless coveted tableware for everyday use from nine outlets around the city.
🚉 H8; alll ✉ Largo do Chiado 20–23 ☎ 213 461 401; www.vistaalegre.pt 🚌 28;
Also at ✉ Rua Castilho 39–5°; ✉ Avenida da Igreja 4f; ✉ Amoreiras Complex Shop No. 2028; ✉ Colombo Complex Shop No. 2080

DECORSÉCULO

One of the Bairro Alto's most interesting shops is Decorséculo in Rua do Século, selling one-off pieces of original designer furniture and household objects.
🚉 H7, H8 ✉ Rua do Século 68 ☎ 213 431 153 🚌 tram 28

ANTIQUES IN LISBON

Whether you are looking for genuine antiques or just bric-a-brac, you will find it in the shops around Rua de São Bento, Rua Dom Pedro, Rua do Alecrim and around the Castelo São Jorge. You will find everything from religious carvings to dolls, together with an array of furniture and items for the home.

Bars & Nightclubs

SOLAR DO VINHO DO PORTO

Owned by the Port Wine Institute, the Solar do Vinho do Porto is a large, relaxed and rather refined bar given over entirely to port. It is one of the places in Lisbon that you should visit at least once. You can order by the glass or bottle from a *lista de vinhos*, which includes over 300 red and white ports. It is in a fine old townhouse in the Bairro Alto, close to the upper station of the Elevador da Glória.
✚ H7 ✉ Rua de São Pedro de Alcântara 45 R/C ☎ 213 475 707 🕓 Mon–Sat 2.30–midnight 🚍 58, 100

HOW MUCH?

In theory, in most top Lisbon clubs there is no official charge at the door but drinks carry a surcharge once inside. In practice, women are rarely asked to pay at the door while the fate of their male companions depends on the mood of the doorman.

ALCÂNTARA MAR

This designer bar is among the smartest and trendiest in Lisbon. After eating in the excellent restaurant cross the little interior bridge to the adjoining, stylish Alcântara-Mar nightclub.
✉ Rua da Cozinha Económica 11 ☎ 213 645 250 🕓 8pm–4am; nightclub open Wed–Sun 🚊 Alcântara (Cascais line) 🚍 12, 20, 22, 28; tram 15

BACHUS

As well as a top restaurant Bachus is one of the city's most refined bars. Oriental carpets, fine furniture and intimate lighting make this popular with Lisbon's glamorous.
✚ H8; alll ✉ Largo da Trindade 8–9 ☎ 213 422 828 🕓 Mon–Fri 12pm–2am 🚇 Baixa-Chiado 🚍 58, 100

CHAPITÔ

A very relaxed and enjoyable outdoor bar by the castle, with good food, an attractive setting and gorgeous views.
✚ J8; clll ✉ Rua Costa do Castelo 1–7 ☎ 218 878 225 🕓 Mon–Sat 🚍 37; tram 12, 28

FRÁGIL

Opened in 1983, this is one of the oldest, most popular and self-consciously trendy of the Bairro's many club-bars.
✚ H8; alll ✉ Rua da Atalaia 128 ☎ 213 469 578 🕓 Mon–Sat 🚍 58, 100; tram 28

KAPITAL

Kapital is so trendy that you have to pass a style test before you can get past the doorman. With three floors of music and bars, plus an excellent rooftop terrace.
✚ G8 ✉ Avenida 24 de Julho 68 ☎ 351 395 5963 🕓 Tue–Sat to 5.30am; Sun–Mon to 4am 🚊 Santos 🚍 14, 28, 32, 40, 43; tram 15, 18

KREMLIN

Almost as hip as Kapital (see above), and almost as difficult to get into, so dress to impress. Gets going after 2am and closes about 7am.
✚ G8 ✉ Escadinhas da Praia 5 ☎ 351 395 7101 🕓 Tue, Thu–Sat 🚊 Santos 🚍 14, 28, 32, 40, 43; tram 15, 18

PLATEAU

If you have no joy at Kremlin (see above), or want something a little less trendy and with more mainstream rock and pop.
✚ G8 ✉ Escadinhas da Praia 7 ☎ 213 965 116 🕓 Tue–Sat 🚊 Santos 🚍 14, 28, 40, 43; tram 15, 18

PAVILHÃO CHINÊS

Covered with a jumble of fans, china, sheet music and other miscellaneous *objets d'art*, the drinks and cocktails here are reasonably priced.
✚ H7 ✉ Rua Dom Pedro V 89 ☎ 213 424 729 🕓 Mon–Sat 6pm–2am; Sun 9pm–2am 🚇 Restauradores 🚍 58, 100

SNOB

A quieter, classier Bairro Alto bar with wooden booths, leather seats and soothing green baize.
✚ H8; alll ✉ Rua da Atalaia-Rua do Século 178 ☎ 213 463 723 🕓 8pm–2am 🚍 58, 100; tram 28

Live Music

ANOS 60
If you want to relive the
1960s this bar, which also
serves light snacks, plays
live music daily. Intimate
and friendly.
🕀 J7; bll–cll ✉ Largo do
Terreirinho 21 ☎ 218 873 444
🕐 Tue–Sat 9.30–4am
🚇 Martim Moniz

BLUES CAFÉ
A former warehouse
midway down the Doca
de Alcântara, near the
heart of the Alcântara
nightlife waterfront
district, is now a bar-club-
restaurant that serves
Cajun food. There is live
blues two or three nights a
week, and DJ dance music
on the other nights.
🕀 G9 ✉ Rua da Cintura do
Porta de Lisboa ☎ 213 957
085 🕐 Tue–Sat 8pm–4am
🚇 Alcântara Mar (Cascais line)
from Cais do Sodré 🚌 27, 28,
29, 43, 49; tram 15

HOT CLUBE JAZZ
This little basement club
has long enjoyed a
reputation as Lisbon's
best place for jazz.
Portuguese and visiting
performers.
🕀 H7; all ✉ Praça de Alegria
39, off Avenida da Liberdade
☎ 213 467 369 🕐 Tue–Wed
for jam sessions, Thu–Sat for
concerts: two sessions 11pm and
12.30am 🚇 Avenida

PAVILHÃO ATLANTICO
& PRAÇA SONY
To the east of the city at
the Expo '98 site, both of
these venues have regular
live music shows and
concerts. Contact the
tourist office for
information or any of the
cities main music shops.

🕀 M1 ✉ Parque das Nações,
Pavilhão do Atlantico ☎ 218
918 409
🕀 M12 ✉ Praça Sony
☎ 218 919 898 🕐 Thu–Sat
10pm–2am 🚇 Oriente

PÉ SUJO
This small club, hidden
away in the Alfama
district, has live Brazilian
samba, *forró* and *batucada*
daily.
🕀 J8; cll ✉ Largo de São
Martinho 6–7 ☎ 218 865 629

RITZ CLUB
A big and buzzy African
club just off Avenida da
Liberdade. Excellent
music from a resident
band or visiting stars.
🕀 H7; all ✉ Rua da Glória 57
☎ 213 425 140 🕐 Mon–Sat
🚇 Restauradores/Avenida
🚌 1, 2, 9, 11, 31 and all other
Avenida da Liberdade services

SALSA LATINA
Near the many restaurants
and bars at the Doca de
Santo Amaro, this club
plays the cities best Latin
sounds, livened up at the
weekends by a live Cuban
band.
🕀 E9 ✉ Antiga Gare Marítima
de Alcântara ☎ 213 950 555
🕐 12–4am 🚇 Alcântara
(Cascais line) 🚌 28

SPEAKEASY
Good quality live jazz
with the occasional big
name is presented two or
three times weekly at this
bar/restaurant at the
eastern end of the Doca
de Alcântara.
🕀 H7; all ✉ Armazém 115,
Cais das Oficinas ☎ 213 957
308 🕐 Mon–Sat 10pm–4am
🚇 Cais do Sodré 🚌 27, 28,
29, 43, 49; tram 15

PLACES
For years you had to go no
further than the streets of the
Bairro Alto to find a good
night out. These days bars and
clubs are increasingly further
afield, because of official
urban regeneration policies
and attempts to take noisy
late-night entertainment away
from the residential Bairro.
Trendy new places have
opened on and around the
Avenida da 24 de Julho (along
the waterfront west of Cais do
Sodré), the Alcântara district
(notably the fast-growing and
increasingly fashionable Doca
do Santo Amaro, also on the
waterfront), and to a lesser
extent the fringes of the
Alfama and Graça districts east
of the heart of the city. Gay
bars and clubs cluster around
the Rato, on the fringes of the
Bairro Alto.

Cinema & Performing Arts

CINEMA

Cinema-going is a pleasure in Lisbon. Unlike those in many European cities, Lisbon cinemas usually show films in their original language, with Portuguese sub-titles. This means that English-speaking visitors can enjoy mainstream Hollywood releases without dubbing. Some cinemas are old-fashioned places, and still have their original art nouveau and art deco interiors. The most popular cinemas tend to be the complexes in the major shopping malls as they have the best sound and quality (▶ 70). Tickets, already low-priced by most visitors' standards, are even cheaper on Mondays, but turn up at the cinema early to be sure of a seat.

ART-HOUSE

Classic films, re-runs and avant-garde movies are shown at a variety of art-house cinemas, most notably the national film theatre:

Instituto da Cinemateca Portuguesa 🚇 H7 ✉ Rua Barata Salgueiro 39 ☎ 213 596 262/266 🎬 Programmes twice daily 🚇 Avenida

MAINSTREAM

The majority of big, first-release films are shown in cinemas clustered around Praça dos Restauradores and off the Avenida da Liberdade. Major first-run cinemas include:

Coliseu 🚇 H7; all ✉ Rua Portas de Santo Antão

☎ 213 240 580
🚇 Restauradores
São Jorge 🚇 H7; all
✉ Avenida da Liberdade 175
☎ 213 103 400
🚇 Restauradores
Vasco da Gama 🚇 M2
✉ Centro Vasco da Gama, Parque das Nações ☎ 218 930 601 🚇 Oriente

CLASSICAL MUSIC

The main driving force behind classical music in Lisbon (and many other cultural activities) is the Fundação Calouste Gulbenkian (Calouste Gulbenkian Foundation). It sponsors its own choir, orchestra and ballet company, and its complex of buildings north of the Parque Eduardo VII has three major concert halls and facilities for outdoor performances. During the October to June season the Foundation presents a wide range of classical and jazz concerts, from small-scale chamber recitals to programmes requiring full symphony orchestras. At other times of the year the Foundation is responsible for all sorts of musical and other events around the city. Programme details can be obtained from the Gulbenkian Museum (▶ 35), which is available in the Foundation complex, or from the tourist office and newspaper listings.

Fundação Calouste Gulbenkian 🚇 G5 ✉ Avenida de Berna 45 ☎ 217 823 000; www.musicagulbenkian.pt 🚇 São Sebastião/Praça de Espanha 🚌 16, 26, 31, 46, 56

TICKETS AND INFORMATION

You can obtain information and tickets for a wide variety of concerts, films, plays and shows by calling in person at the Agência de Bilhetes para Espectáculos Públicos (ABEP), on the corner of Praça dos Restauradores (☎ 213 475 824). Tickets are also available from the ticket office in FNAC in the Armezéns do Chiado Shopping Centre at Rua do Carmo 2. The tourist office in the same square publishes the *Agenda Cultural*, a free monthly listings magazine. The Museu Calouste Gulbenkian issues details of its own programme of events. The local *Diário de Notícias* and *O Independente* newspapers carry listings (in Portuguese) and the Friday editions carry free pull-out listings supplements. The Centro Cultural de Belém also issues monthly listings booklets for its own events.

OTHER CONCERT VENUES

A full range of classical music performances are held in the Teatro Nacional de São Carlos and Teatro Municipal de São Luís. Recitals are also given in the two auditoria in the Centro Cultural de Belém out in the western suburb of Belém.

Teatro Nacional de São Carlos ✚ H8; aIII–aIV ✉ Rua Serpa Pinto 9 ☎ 213 253 000; www.saocarlos.pt 🕐 Box office: daily 1–7 🚇 Baixo-Chiado 🚌 100, 58; tram 28

Teatro Municipal de São Luís ✚ H8; aIII–aIV ✉ Rua António Maria Cardoso 40 ☎ 213 427 172 🚇 Baixa-Chiado 🚌 58, 100; tram 28

Centro Cultural de Belém ✚ B10 ✉ Praça do Império ☎ 213 612 400; www.ccb.pt 🚆 Belém (Cascais line from Cais do Sodré) 🚌 29, 43; tram 15

In summer, concerts are held throughout the city (many of them free), particularly in churches, including:
Sé (the cathedral, ➤ 44)
São Roque (➤ 38)
Basílica da Estrela (➤ 34)
São Vicente de Fora (➤ 57)
The ruined Convento do Carmo, now the Museu Arqueológico do Carmo (➤ 40)
Igreja dos Mártires, Rua Garrett in the Chiado.

OPERA AND BALLET

Lisbon's principal opera and ballet performances take place in the beautiful 18th-century Teatro Nacional de São Carlos and the adjacent Teatro Municipal de São Luís in the Bairro Alto. Note that neither the opera nor the ballet season extends right through the summer: Typically the seasons run from mid-September to July. The Calouste Gulbenkian Foundation has its own ballet company and facilities for indoor and outdoor performances. Opera and ballet are among the events held at the Centro Cultural de Belém (see above).

THEATRE

The performing arts in Lisbon are enjoying more popularity than ever with young people involved both as spectators and performers. Most of Lisbon's theatre performances are in Portuguese. However, you can sample the traditional musical revues without a grasp of the language. Small theatres are dotted across the city; the main performance space is the Rossio's eye-catching Teatro Nacional de Dona Maria II, completed in 1846. Many performances are in the Coliseu complex.

Teatro Nacional Dona Maria ✚ H8; bII ✉ Praça Dom Pedro IV (Rossio) ☎ 213 422 210 or 213 250 800 🚇 Rossio 🚌 1, 2, 31, 36, 41 and all Rossio services

Coliseu ✚ H7; aII ✉ Rua Portas de Santo Antão ☎ 213 240 580 🚇 Restauradores

SINTRA MUSIC FESTIVAL

Each year in June and July, a series of concerts, ballet performances and other events are held in palaces and country houses in and around Sintra. Venues include the Palácio Nacional in Sintra (➤ 21), the gorgeous pink palace of Queluz, and the palace at Seteias, now a luxury hotel (➤ 86). Details from the tourist information office in Lisbon (➤ 91) or Sintra (➤ 21).

Fado

COVER CHARGE

Fado houses don't charge admission, but nearly all make a cover charge. This usually buys you a couple of drinks. Performances usually start around 9pm, the real action may begin to hot up only between 11pm and midnight. The price guides for restaurants shown on this page indicate the cost of a meal (➤ 64).

HISTORY OF FADO

Lisbon and Coimbra are the two great cites of fado—a melancholy form of traditional singing accompanied by guitar. Passion, fate and regrets are the main themes. It may originate from African slave songs, or have Moorish roots. In Lisbon the singer (*fadista*) is nearly always a woman, and is accompanied by one or two impassive male guitarists. Coimbra fado is sung by men, and has a less heartrending quality.

THE REAL THING

Sadly, as with many traditional forms of culture, some old clubs have been smartened up and the music stripped of its soul for the benefit of tourists. Try to steer clear of places that have uniformed staff on the door and where photographers hustle to sell you pictures of you taken at your table.

ADEGA DO MACHADO (€€)

Once one of the oldest and among the most revered of all the fado clubs in Portugal, where now you can experience fado and folk dancing in traditional costume, albeit rather touristy.

➕ H8; all‖ ✉ Rua do Norte 91 ☎ 213 224 640 🕐 Tue–Sun 8pm–3am 🚇 Baixa-Chiado 🚌 58, 100; tram 28

ADEGA DO RIBATEJO (€€)

Popular with locals, there are fado performances by paid singers and also by the cooks or the management.

➕ H8; all‖ ✉ Rua Diário de Notícias 23 ☎ 213 468 343 🕐 Mon–Sat 8pm–2am 🚇 Baixi-Chiado 🚌 58, 100; tram 28

A SEVERA (€€€)

Named after a legendary 19th-century gypsy *fadista*, it attracts many of the big names in the fado firmament and charges high prices.

➕ H8; all‖ ✉ Rua das Gáveas 51 ☎ 213 428 314 🕐 Fri–Wed 8pm–3 🚇 Baixi-Chiado 🚌 58, 100; tram 28

LISBOA A NOITE (€€€)

One of the more touristy of the city's fado houses. It is fine if you want to eat and listen in comfortable surroundings, but not if you want the rough-edged authenticity of a genuine club and real fado.

➕ H8; all‖ ✉ Rua das Gáveas 69 ☎ 213 468 557 🕐 Mon–Sat 8pm–3 🚇 Baixi-Chiado 🚌 58, 100; tram 28 ❓ Performances start at 9.30pm

O SENHOR VINHO (€€€)

In Lapa, this celebrated club is some way to the west of the tourist haunts of the Alfama and Bairro Alto. As a result it is far more authentic—though not necessarily much cheaper—than many other clubs.

➕ G8 ✉ Rua do Meio à Lapa 18 ☎ 213 972 681 🕐 Mon–Sat 8.30pm–2.30am 🚌 13, 27; tram 25, 28

PARREIRINHA DA ALFAMA (€€)

Another of the city's more venerable clubs with some of the century's greatest names in fado. Both the cover charge and food prices are lower than those of its big-name rivals. No dancing.

➕ J8; cll‖ ✉ Beco do Espírito Santo 1, off Largo do Chafariz de Dentro ☎ 218 868 209 🕐 Mon–Sat 8–2am 🚌 37; tram 28

RESTAURANTE SÃO CAETANO (€€)

Worth visiting for the food as well as the fado, with an authentic non-touristy atmosphere.

➕ F8 ✉ Rua de São Caetano à Lapa 27 ☎ 213 974 792 🕐 Mon–Fri lunch, dinner; Sat, Sun dinner only 🚌 13, 27; tram 25

TIMPANAS (€€)

The show in this fado house in the Alcântara district is organised with dinner and folk dancing rather than spontaneous fado, but there's still some good singing.

➕ F9 ✉ Rua Gilberto Rola 🚇 213 906 655 🚉 Alcântara Mar 🚌 27, 40, 49, 60; tram 15, 18

Sport & Leisure

BULLFIGHTS

Bullfighting is every bit as popular in Portugal as in Spain, and though less gory than in Spain as the Portuguese concentrate on fine horsemanship, it also involves taunting and weakening the bull by spearing it with *banderilhas* (lances decorated with ribbons) and then killing it (but not in the ring). The spectacle is not for everyone. Bullfights take place on various dates between Easter and September at Portugal's largest ring, the Praça de Touros do Campo Pequeno. Call for details.

🚻 H4 ✉ Avenida João XXI–Avenida da República ☎ 212 932 442 🚇 Campo Pequeno

GOLF

Lisbon Sports Club has a course at Belas, 18 km north of Lisbon (☎ 214 321 474). Robert Trent Jones has designed courses at Quinta da Marinha, west of Cascais (☎ 214 833 378); Penha Longha, between Estoril and Sintra (☎ 219 249 011); and Aroeira near Almada, south of Lisbon (☎ 212 979 100).

SOCCER

Lisbon, like the rest of Portugal, is soccer (football) mad. The city's two main teams are Benfica and Sporting. Benfica is based at the giant Estádio da Luz and Sporting's home is the Estádio José Alvalade. Tickets for games (held on Sunday afternoon or evening) can be bought at the grounds, but for big games such as matches between the two local teams, or visits from F C Porto, it is best to try and buy tickets in advance from the booth in Praça dos Restauradores.

Benfica 🚻 E3 www.slbenfica.pt 🚇 Colégio Militar Luz
Sporting 🚻 G2 www.sporting.pt 🚇 Campo Grande

SWIMMING

In summer locals head for the beaches at Cascais, a former fishing village, the elegant old royal town Estoril and Carcavelos. The towns' beaches stretch some 20km west of the city (the town beaches are not recommended for swimming). They can be easily reached by regular direct trains from Cais do Sodré (some services change at Oeiras). The Guincho beach, which has a huge Atlantic swell, is known for its surfing but is dangerous at night as people have been robbed at knife point. There are also several hotel pools, including Lapa Palace (▶ 86), and public pools within the city limits.

TENNIS

Several major Lisbon hotels have tennis courts, some open to non-patrons. Otherwise it is usually possible to play at one of the city's many public courts. Most accessible of these are in the Alvalade (Lisboa Racket Centre) and at Estádio 1 de Maio. Contact the tourist office for details.

🚻 J3 ✉ Praça de Alvalade 🚇 Alvalade
🚻 J3–J4 ✉ Estádio 1 de Maio 🚇 Roma

CASINO

Europe's largest casino, owned by the multimillionaire Stanley Ho has live shows along with fine dining in its world-famous Chinese restaurant, and world-class gambling facilities at its prime location in front of the sea at Estoril.

🚻 Off map ☎ 214 667 700 🕐 Daily 3pm–3am 🚇 Estoril on Cascais line from Cais do Sodré

JOGGING

If you fancy a run during the day you could head for the Parque Eduardo VII (avoid at night–reports of muggings) but better perhaps is the newly finished promenade linking the Doca de San to Marao to Belém. Pick up the train at either end.

🚇 Alcântara/Belém 🚌 28

Expensive Hotels

PRICES

Approximate prices per night for a double room:
Expensive over €200
Mid-Range €100–200
Budget under €100

BOOKING

Book a room well in advance if you plan to visit Lisbon over Easter or during mid-summer. At other times it is safest to book, but some sort of accomoodation can usually be found on arrival. The information desk at the main Portela Airport has details of day-to-day availability but cannot make bookings for you. The city's main tourist offices will also supply lists of accommodation.

AS JANELAS VERDES

An intimate 17-room hotel in an 18th-century townhouse with spacious and sump-tuously fitted rooms. The location means the front rooms can be noisy.

➕ G9 ✉ Rua das Janelas Verdes 47 ☎ 213 968 143; fax 213 968 144; www.heritage.pt 🚌 40, 49, 60; tram 27

AVENIDA PALACE

This is the place to choose if you want a traditional hotel at the heart of the city. Built in 1842 and recently refurbished, it lies between the busy Rossio and Praça dos Restauradores, but the rooms away from the street are calm, comfortable and spacious.

➕ H8; all ✉ Rua 1 de Dezembro 123 ☎ 213 460 151; fax 213 422 884; www.hotel-avenida-palace.pt 🚇 Rossio

LAPA PALACE

This 94-room five-star hotel is one of Lisbon's newest and most expensive. It is in a 19th-century palace and a modern six-storey block with luxurious rooms. Lovely garden with pool.

➕ F8 ✉ Rua do Pau de Bandeira 4 ☎ 213 949 494; fax 213 950 665; www.lapa-palace.com 🚌 13; tram 27

METROPOLE

An imposing and elegant building in the Rossio—central but also noisy. Air conditioning and double glazing help.

➕ H8; blll ✉ Praça Dom Pedro IV 30 ☎ 213 469 164; fax 213 469 166 🚇 Rossio

RITZ FOUR SEASONS

Lisbon's most famous de luxe hotel since it opened in the 1950s. All 310 rooms have their own balconies.

➕ H6 ✉ Rua Rodrigo do Fonseca 88 ☎ 213 811 400; fax 213 831 783; www.fourseasons.com 🚇 Marquês de Pombal 🚌 1, 2, 9, 11, 31 and all other Avenida da Liberdade services

SOFITEL LISBOA

One of the city's newest luxury options, with 163 rooms, this hotel is stylish and modern and appeals to business travellers as well as tourists.

➕ H7 ✉ Avenida da Liberdade 123 ☎ 213 228 300; fax 213 228 310; www.sofitel.com 🚇 Avenida 🚌 1, 2, 9, 11, 31 and all other Avenida da Liberdade services

YORK HOUSE

Well west of the heart of the city. However, this is one of Lisbon's most popular hotels, with a lovely tree- and plant-filled courtyard, and 34 simple but tasteful rooms.

➕ G8 ✉ Rua das Janelas 32 ☎ 213 962 435; fax 213 972 793; www.yorkhouselisboa.com 🚌 27, 40, 49, 60; tram 25

SINTRA

PALÁCIO DE SETEAIS

A sumptuous 30-room hotel in a lovely 19th-century palace, with period furnishings. The views are all that you could wish of Sintra.

➕ Off map ✉ Rua Barbosa do Bocage 10, 2710 Sintra ☎ 219 233 200; fax 219 234 277; www.tivolihotels.com 🚇 Sintra

Mid-Range Hotels

BRITÂNIA

A traditional, 30-room, hotel built in 1944 on a pleasant street one block east of the Avenida da Liberdade. Rooms were refurbished in 1995, but retain old-fashioned charm and its art deco interior. Courteous service. Breakfast is the only meal served.

➕ H7 ✉ Rua Rodrigues Sampaio 17 ☎ 213 155 016; fax 213 155 021; www.heritage/pt 🚇 Avenida 🚌 1, 2, 9, 11, 31 and all other Avenida da Liberdade services

CASA DE SÃO MAMEDE

This homely and pleasantly traditional pension is by the Jardim Botânico (➤ 58) on the northern fringes of the Bairro Alto. The 28 rooms are simple, but pleasantly furnished.

➕ G7 ✉ Rua da Escola Politécnica 159 ☎ 213 963 166; fax 213 951 896 🚇 Avenida 🚌 10, 20, 24, 29, 30

EXECUTIVE

Modern hotel but small and very prettily fitted out. It is close to the Gulbenkian—not central but with good transport to central Lisbon. Breakfast served but no restaurant.

➕ H5 ✉ Avenida Cibde de Valbom 56–62 ☎ 217 951 157; fax 217 951 166 🚇 S Sebastião 🚌 16, 18, 26, 42, 46, 56

HOTEL JORGE V

This 1960s building is just off the Avenida da Liberdade, close to the heart of the city. Small rooms but nice balconies for breakfast and tea.

➕ G7–H7 ✉ Rua Mouzinho da Silveira 3 ☎ 213 562 525; fax 213 150 319; www.hoteljorgev.com 🚇 Marquês de Pombal 🚌 all Avenida de Liberdade services

MIRAPARQUE

An almost perfect mid-range friendly hotel on a quiet tree-lined street overlooking the Parque Eduardo VII and Pavilhão dos Desportos. Rooms are a little dated, but large, bright and spotlessly clean. Serves good Portuguese food. Only a minute from the metro.

➕ H6 ✉ Avenida Sidónio Pais 12 ☎ 213 524 286; fax 213 578 920; www.miraparque.com 🚇 Parque

SENHORA DO MONTE

This lovely hilltop hotel in the Graça district, north of the Castelo, would be the first choice in its category if it were closer to the inner city. It has 28 very attractive rooms, some with balconies and air-conditioning, and a relaxed and amiable ambience. No restaurant, but breakfast is served.

➕ J7 ✉ Calçada do Monte 39 ☎ 218 866 002; fax 218 877 783 🚇 Martim Moniz 🚌 7, 8, 40; tram 12, 17,28, 35

SINTRA

CENTRAL

Right in the middle of town, looking towards the palace, the Central has 11 rooms with a bath.

➕ Off map ✉ Largo Rainha D Amélia, Sintra-Vila ☎ 219 230 963 🚇 Sintra

WHERE TO STAY

Of the more expensive hotels, the older ones tend to be close to the Rossio, while the newer establishments are in the north on, or just off, the Avenida da Liberdade. Other choice hotels are in residential suburbs well away from the heart of the city, mostly in the west or northeast. Most budget options are near the Rossio and in the Baixa, but these central locations are likely to be noisy unless you can secure an off-street room. Two of the city's most picturesque places to stay, the atmospheric Bairro Alto and Alfama districts, have relatively few hotels.

Budget Accommodation

NOISE

Lisbon is notoriously noisy. Expensive hotels are not immune to the cacophony, but most have double-glazing and air-conditioning, which provide a measure of protection. Cheaper hotels are usually not so blessed, and may be near the Rossio, Baixa or Bairro Alto, three of the city's busier districts. Try to avoid rooms on the street, and check for bars or restaurants nearby which are likely to be open until the small hours.

USEFUL TIPS

If you are searching for cheap accommodation under your own steam remember that many pensions are in buildings that look much more run down from the outside than they are inside. Many cheaper places are on the upper floors of blocks, so note the address carefully. In Lisbon a street number is often followed by the floor number: 74–3°, for example, means the property is at number 74 in the street and on the third floor.

HOTEL BORGES

A comfortable if unexceptional hotel worth staying at as it is close to the Chiado shopping district. Popular, so book ahead.
✚ H8; alll ✉ Rua Garrett 108–10 ☎ 213 461 951; fax 213 426 617; www.hotelborges.com 🚇 Baixa-Chiado 🚊 tram 28

PENSÃO GALICIA

On the fourth floor of a block between the Baixa and Chiado districts, in the street immediately west of the Baixa's Rua Áurea. Although all the rooms are smallish, some have balconies.
✚ J8; blll ✉ Rua do Crucifixio 50–54 ☎ 213 428 430 🚇 Baixa-Chiado

PENSÃO LONDRES

This friendly and efficient pension in an old townhouse is plusher than most in its price category. Rooms vary considerably; some on the fourth floor have views, so look first.
✚ H7 ✉ Rua Dom Pedro V 53–2° ☎ 213 462 203; fax 213 465 682; www. pensaolondres.com 🚌 58, 100

PENSÃO NINHO DAS ÁGUIAS

Not all the rooms in the 'Eagle's Nest' have views, but every guest can enjoy the panorama from the tower of this pension in the Alfama beneath the Castelo.
✚ J8; bll ✉ Costa do Castelo 74 ☎ 218 854 070; no fax 🚌 Tram 12

PENSÃO SÃO JOÃO DE PRAÇA

An amiable pension in a pleasant townhouse in Alfama, immediately east of the cathedral. Rooms, all on the second floor, are clean.
✚ J8; clll ✉ Rua São João da Praça 97–2° ☎ 218 862 591; fax 218 880 415 🚌 37; tram 28

POUSADA DE JUVENTUDE DE LISBOA

Lisbon's 200-bed youth hostel has private double rooms as well as dormitory accommodation. The hostel is open all day, and there is no curfew.
✚ H6 ✉ Rua Andrade Corvo 46 ☎ 213 532 696; fax 213 537 541 🚇 Picoas

RESIDENCIAL CAMÕES

A perfect location in the Bairro Alto is the main selling point of this friendly first-floor *residencial*. Small, attractive rooms and nice communal areas. The more expensive rooms have balconies and/or private bathrooms.
✚ H8; alll ✉ Travessa do Poço da Cidade 38–2° ☎ 213 467 510; fax 213 464 058 🚇 Rossio /Baixa-Chiado 🚌 58, 100

SÉ GUESTHOUSE

This welcoming guesthouse is in the same pleasant and well-located townhouse as the Pensão São João da Praça (see above). Bathrooms are shared, but the light and airy rooms are a touch smarter than its near neighbour, and all have TVs. A good breakfast is included in the room rate.
✚ J8; alll ✉ Costa do Castelo 74 ☎ 218 854 070; no fax 🚌 Tram 12

LISBON
travel facts

ESSENTIAL FACTS

Customs regulations

- Provided it is for personal use, EU nationals can bring back as much as they like, although the following guidelines should be adhered to: 800 cigarettes, 400 cigarillos, 200 cigars, 1 kg tobacco; 10 litres of spirits, 20 litres of fortified wine, 90 litres of wine, 110 litres of beer.

Electricity

- Current is 220 volts AC (50 cycles), but is suitable for 240 volt appliances. Plugs are of the two-round-pin variety.

Etiquette

- Do not wear shorts, mini skirts or skimpy tops in churches, and do not intrude during services.
- Do not eat or drink in churches. Many churches forbid the use of flash and some ban photography.
- Always be respectful, especially towards people in authority.
- There are few non-smoking areas, but smoking is banned on public transport (including boats).

Lavatories

- Public toilets (*lavabos*) are few.
- Men's toilets are marked *homens*, women's *senhoras*. *Quarto de banho* means 'bathroom'.
- You can usually use café and hotel toilets without being a customer; otherwise use toilets at bus and train stations.
- To ask 'where is the toilet', say *'onde ficam os lavabos?'*

Money matters

- Foreign exchange bureaux (*cambios*) and banks with exchange facilities are generally open Mon–Fri 8.30–3. You can also change money at the airport and Santa Apolónia railway station (24-hour services), the main post office and automatic exchange machines. Automatic Teller Machines (ATMs), or Multibanco, give credit card cash advances.
- Commission rates on travellers' cheques are often high. Savings banks or building societies (*caixas*) may charge cheaper rates. It is best to look around.
- Credit cards are widely accepted.

Opening times

- Shops: 🕒 Mon–Fri 9/9.30/10–12.30/1, 2.30/3–7/8. Many shops close for the weekend at 1pm on Saturday.
- Malls: May remain open very late, seven days a week.
- Banks: 🕒 Mon–Fri 8.30–2.45/3. Some exchange facilities in the evening.
- Post offices: 🕒 Mon–Fri 8.30–6. Larger branches occasionally open Sat 9–noon
- Restaurants: Lunch is usually served noon–3, dinner from 7.30.
- Museums: 🕒 10–12.30 and 2–6. Important museums may remain open all day but times vary. Most are closed on Mondays.
- Churches: 🕒 7–noon and 4–7. Some open only for early morning and evening services.

Places of worship

- Anglican: St. George's Church ✉ Jardim da Estrela, Rua de São Jorge 6 🕒 Service Sun 11.45am
- Baptist: Igreja Evangelica Baptista de Lisboa ✉ Rua Filipe Folque 36b ☎ 213 535 362
- Roman Catholic mass in English: Dominican Church of Corpo Santo ✉ Largo do Corpo Santo 32 🕒 Service Sun 11am
- Presbyterian: St. Andrew's Church of Scotland ✉ Rua Arriaga 13 🕒 Service Sun 11am
- Jewish: Shaare Tikau Synagogue ✉ Rua Alexandre Herculano 59 ☎ 213 881 592

Public holidays

- 1 Jan: New Year's Day; Good Friday; 25 Apr: Liberation Day; 1 May: May Day; Corpus Christi (late May or early Jun); 10 Jun: Camões Day; 13 Jun: St. Anthony's Day; 15 Aug: Assumption; 5 Oct: Republic Day; 1 Nov: All Saints' Day; 1 Dec: Independence Day; 8 Dec: Immaculate Conception; 25 Dec: Christmas Day

Students and senior travellers

- Certain museums give discounts to student and senior travellers. Discounted coach and rail travel are available on production of an under-26 youth card.

Tourist Card

- The highly recommended Lisbon Tourist Card (*Lisboa Card*) gives free admittance to virtually all city museums and other attractions, and free or discounted use of public transport (except trams 15 and 28, and the Santa Justa elevator). There is also a 65 per cent discount on the Aerobus airport shuttle. It is valid for 24, 48 or 72 hours (prices to April 2005 €13.25/22.50/27.50), and is sold at many outlets, including the tourist offices lited below. Children pay a reduced price. Pre-paid taxi vouchers and a 24- and 72-hour Shopping Card, and 72-hour Restaurant Card are also available. The last two provide discounts at a limited number of selected shops and restaurants.

Tourist information

- Main offices: Lisboa Welcome Center ✉ Praça do Comércio ☎ 210 312 810 🕐 Daily 9–8; Palácio Foz ✉ Praça dos Restauradores ☎ 213 463 314 🕐 Daily 9–8
- There are other offices or kiosks at Artesanto do Tejo ✉ Rua do Arsenal 25 ☎ 210 312 850 🕐 Daily 9/10–8; Santa Apolónia railway station ☎ 218 821 606 🕐 Summer Mon–Sat 9–8, winter Wed–Sat 8–1; Bélem ✉ Monasteiro dos Jerónimos ☎ 213 658 435 🕐 Summer daily 9–7, winter Tue–Sat 10–1, 2–6; Calle Augusta ☎ 213 259 131 🕐 Summer daily 9–7, winter daily 10–1, 2–6; Portela airport ☎ 218 450 660 🕐 Daily 8am–midnight

GETTING AROUND

Buses, trams and elevators

- The Elevador de Santa Justa runs from Rua Áurea (Rua do Ouro) in the Baixa to Largo do Carmo in the Bairro Alto.
- The Elevador da Glória funicular runs from Praça dos Restauradores to Rua São Pedro de Alcântara in the Bairro Alto. The Elevador da Bica goes from Rua de São Paulo to Largo Calhariz-Rua do Loreto.
- You can buy single journey or cheaper two-journey tickets, or a book of 10 tickets (*módulos* or *caderneta*), which is cheaper still.
- Tickets can be bought from machines (not from the driver) on the new large trams (notably the 15). You must have the right coins.
- Show pre-bought tickets and passes to the driver or validate them in the machines on board.
- One-day or three-day bus, lift and tram passes, or three-day bus, tram, lifts and metro passes are available. Validate a pass the first time you use it: 24-hour or 72-hour validity starts from that time.
- A Tourist Pass (*Passe Turístico*) gives unlimited travel for four days or seven days on buses, trams, metro and elevators. It is available on production of a passport at carris kiosks including those near the Santa Justa elevator (close to the Rossio), in Praça da Figueira and the Restauradores Metro station.

91

Metro

- A discounted ten-ticket *caderneta* and one- and seven-day Metro-only passes are available. Validate the pass on your first journey.
- Services run 6.30am–1am.
- Metro information from tourist offices (► 91) or the website (► 5).

Taxis

- Taxi ranks are on the Rossio, Praça da Figueira and else-where; or phone ☎ 218 155 061, 217 932 756 or 218 152 076
- Fares are 20 per cent higher between 10pm and 6am, at week-ends and during public holidays. A charge of €1.50 may be added when the boot is used for luggage over a designated size.

MEDIA & COMMUNICATIONS

Postal services

- Post offices are *correios*. Letter boxes are red.
- Lisbon's main post office (Correio Geral) is at Praça do Comércio ➕ J8; blV ☎ 213 220 900 🕐 Mon–Fri 8.30–6.30. Its *poste restante* service is at Rua do Arsenal 27 🕐 Mon–Fri 9–2
- There is another large office on Praça dos Restauradores ➕ H7; all ✉ Rua Jardim do Regedor 50 🕐 Mon–Fri 8am–8pm; Sat–Sun 9–6
- Other post offices usually open Mon–Fri 8 or 9–6. Smaller offices may open 8 or 9–12.30 and 2.30–6. Main offices may open on Saturday morning.
- Buy stamps (*selos*) at post offices or shops displaying the sign 'CTT Selos' or 'Correio de Portugal Selos'.
- Current prices for postcards and letters are 30c (EU), 70c other for-eign destinations).
- Air mail is *por avião*. The quickest express service is Correio Azul.

Telephones

- The Lisbon area code is 21 and must be dialled regardless of where you call from. It is followed by a seven-digit number. Numbers in this guide are given inclusive of this area code.
- Telecom pay phones are found in bars, cafés, tourist offices and newsagents.
- Public phones accept all euro coins.
- Public phones increasingly accept TLP or Credifone phone cards (available from most post offices in euro denominations).
- Most post offices (► 92) have phone booths: tell the clerk where you want to call and pay when you have finished.
- Long-distance calls can be incon-venient to make from coin pay phones. It is best to use a Credifone or post office booth instead. There are no cheap periods for international calls from public telephones.
- English-speaking operator for reverse charge (collect) calls abroad, or dialling problems ☎ 171 (Europe and intercontinental). Information on international calls ☎ 179 National Directory ☎ 118
- To call the UK from Portugal, dial 0044. To call Portugal from the UK, dial 00351
- To call the US from Portugal dial 001. To call Portugal from the US dial 99351

EMERGENCIES

Emergency phone numbers

- General emergencies ☎ 112
- Main police station ➕ H8; alll ✉ Rua Capelo 13 ☎ 213 466 141 or tourist police ☎ 213 143 324 🕐 24 hours Report crime and theft here to make a claim on your insurance.
- Red Cross/Ambulance ☎ 219 421 111

Embassies

- Canada ✚ H7 ✉ Avenida da Liberdade
144–156 – 4° ☎ 213 476 466 🕐 Mon–Fri
8.30–12.30, 1.30–5 🚇 Avenida
- United Kingdom ✚ G7 ✉ Rua de São
Bernardo 33 ☎ 213 924 000 🕐 Mon–Fri 9–1,
2.30–5.30 🚌 13, 27; tram 28
- United States ✚ G4 ✉ Avenida das
Forças Armadas ☎ 217 273 300 🕐 Mon–Fri 8–5
🚇 Sete Rios/Entrecampos

Lost property

- Police lost property office ✚ J6/7; bl
✉ Praça Cidade Salazar Lote 180 R/C, Olivais
☎ 218 535 403 🕐 Mon–Fri 9–noon, 2–6
🚌 10, 31 🚇 Olivais
- Buses and trams ✚ H8; blll ✉ Rua de
Santa Justa 11 🕐 Mon–Sat 3–7 ☎ 213 427 944
on the day, if not contact police (above) 🚇 Rossio
- Metro ✚ H7; all ✉ Marques do Pombal
Metro, North atrium ☎ 217 980 600, 213 558 457
or 213 500 100

Medical and dental treatment

- Consult your hotel for details of
local doctors or call the British
Hospital for advice (see below).
- British Hospital: Most staff here
speak English, but there is no
casualty department ✚ F7/G7 ✉ Rua
Saraiva de Carvalho 49 ☎ 213 943 100, 213 943
133 or 213 943 115 🚌 9; tram 25, 28
- Details of pharmacies 24-hour rota
services are posted on pharmacy
doors and in local newspapers.
Normal opening is Mon–Fri 9–1,
2–7; Sat 9–1.

Sensible precautions

- Don't carry large amounts of cash;
use credit cards or travellers'
cheques.
- Never wear expensive jewellery.
- Be on your guard against pickpockets on crowded buses, in
markets and in streets, and beware
of strap-cutting thieves.
- Avoid the port, railway station,
parks and the Alfama after dark.

LANGUAGE

Portuguese is a Romance language,
so a knowledge of French, Spanish or
Italian will help you decipher the
written word. The spoken word is a
different thing. The pronunciation is
difficult, at least at the outset.

Basics

yes/no	sim/não
please	por favour
thank you	obrigado (said by a man), obrigada (said by a woman)
hello	olá
goodbye	adeus
good morning	bom dia
good afternoon	boa tarde
good night	boa noite
excuse me	com licença
I'm sorry	desculpe
how much	quanto
where	onde
big/little	grande/pequeno
cheap	barato
expensive	caro
today	hoje
tomorrow	amanhã
yesterday	ontem
open/closed	aberto/fechado
men	homens
women	senhoras
I don't understand	não compreendo
How much is it?	quanto custa?
At what time…?	a que horas?
Please help me	ajude-me por favor
Do you speak English?	fala Inglês?

1	um	9	nove
2	dois	10	dez
3	três	20	vinte
4	quatro	21	vinte e um
5	cinco	50	cinquenta
6	seis	100	cem
7	sete	101	cento e um
8	oito	1,000	mil

Index

AA CITYPack
Lisbon

It's up to date and easy to use.

Expert travel writer Tim Jepson tells you all you need to know about Lisbon.

Top 25 Sights

"The separate map in AA CityPack is brilliant"
You Magazine, Mail on Sunday

- Top 25 sights in Lisbon

Shopping

- The best of the rest

- Restaurants – all prices and cuisines

- Living Lisbon – the magazine

- The best walks

Eating Out

- Music, nightclubs, theatres, bars

- Shopping choices

- Street map and index

Nightlife

The AA's travel experts have created this guide to help you make the most of your trip. Visit www.theAA.com/bookshop for more AA travel information.

Just **AA** *sk...*

Street Map

ISBN 0-7495-4356-6

£6.99